Two for the
SUMMIT

Two for the
SUMMIT

My Daughter,
the Mountains,
and Me

Geoffrey Norman

A DUTTON BOOK

DUTTON
Published by the Penguin Group
Penguin Putnam Inc., 375 Hudson Street, New York, New York 10014, U.S.A.
Penguin Books Ltd, 27 Wrights Lane, London W8 5TZ, England
Penguin Books Australia Ltd, Ringwood, Victoria, Australia
Penguin Books Canada Ltd, 10 Alcorn Avenue, Toronto, Ontario, Canada M4V 3B2
Penguin Books (N.Z.) Ltd, 182–190 Wairau Road, Auckland 10, New Zealand

Penguin Books Ltd, Registered Offices: Harmondsworth, Middlesex, England

First published by Dutton, a member of Penguin Putnam Inc.

First Printing, August, 2000
10 9 8 7 6 5 4 3 2 1

Portions of this book first appeared in a slightly different form in *National Geographic Adventure* magazine.

REGISTERED TRADEMARK—MARCA REGISTRADA

LIBRARY OF CONGRESS CATALOGING-IN-PUBLICATION DATA:

Norman, Geoffrey.
    Two for the summit : my daughter, the mountains, and me / by Geoffrey Norman.
        p.   cm.
    ISBN 0-525-94494-X
    1. Rock climbing. 2. Fathers and daughters. 3. Norman, Geoffrey. 4. Norman, Brooke.
I. Title.
GV200.2.N67 2000
796.52'23'092—dc21
[B]   00-023993

Printed in the United States of America
Set in Century Expanded
Designed by Eve L. Kirch

This book is printed on acid-free paper. ∞

For Marsha, Brooke, and Hadley.
The ladies in my life

CONTENTS

ACKNOWLEDGMENTS

I got a lot of help in the mountains from the kind of people who make climbing an unselfish enterprise, full of a wonderful spirit of camaraderie. I hope that I have mentioned them all in the text. Back in town, I got even more help from three people who are not mentioned in the text. A wise editor named Elisa Petrini signed up the book. Another wise editor named Jennifer Kasius worked on the manuscript and made it better. And, finally, my agent and friend for 20 years, Amanda Urban, came up with the idea. Plainly, I am lucky with the ladies.

Two for the
SUMMIT

Our Big One

At night, in my dream, I stoutly climbed a mountain,
Going out along with my staff of holly-wood.
                              —Po-Chu-i, A.D. 772–846

We had been walking for about an hour, with a three-day trek ahead of us to base camp. This was the easy part. The weather was good and we had fresh legs. Our packs were light and we would be gaining around 1,500 feet of altitude a day. We were starting at about 9,000 feet, and base camp was at about 13,500. We could not see the mountain we had come here to climb, wouldn't get our first look at it until the end of the second day of the trek, so it all seemed a little theoretical . . . until our first meeting with a climber on his way out.

He was wearing navy blue polypropylene underwear over a pair of khaki shorts, with Tevas on his feet and a gimmie hat on his head. Sunglasses and a two-week beard covered his face. He was riding a mule, very ungracefully, and muttering, over and over, through blistered lips: "I couldn't make it. I just couldn't make it." It was hard to tell who he was talking to. It could have been the mule. The man was just a little short of delirious, and you felt like you should look away from him, the way you do when you encounter one of those deranged street people.

A horse-mounted gaucho accompanied the defeated climber, and he seemed sublimely indifferent to the man's laments. But they made a deep impression on me.

"What have I gotten us into?" I said to myself. Words that would become my mantra for the next three weeks.

The "us" part was critical. If I had come here alone, then I could have made the summit of the mountain or not, suffered or not, lost fingers and toes or not, even died or not (unlikely, though 16 people had perished on this mountain a year earlier), and it wouldn't have been a big deal even in my own mind. I had a long history of doing stupid things—I liked to think of them as stunts—and felt like I pretty much deserved what I got. But my daughter was with me this time. A parent always feels responsible for a child's misfortune, even when he is utterly blameless. But in this case, if anything happened to Brooke, any guilt I felt would be richly deserved.

But where I'd seen an omen (and maybe myself) mounted on that mule, to Brooke it had merely been a middle-aged man who couldn't cut it. I watched as she moved out ahead of me with the rest of our group. There was confidence in the way she walked and youth in the way she carried her pack, and I think I must have been hoping that it would still be there three weeks from now—after we had summited and come down off the mountain.

If we made the summit—and after our meeting with the man on the mule, I had my doubts—it would be the glory of an odd, but spirited little climbing partnership. Brooke and I had been climbing only for five years, and for both of us, climbing was something we did when we could steal the time. But we were eager and passionate about climbing, and we talked about it a lot, about climbs we had made and some we still hoped to make. We had done almost all of our climbing together. We were, in the jargon, "climbing buddies."

It had been our ambition (mine especially) to make one big,

expeditionary climb together someday, and in early 1999 we had our chance. Now we were in Argentina, on a three-day approach up glacial riverbeds to our base camp. From there, we would try for the summit of Aconcagua.

At 22,834 feet, Aconcagua is the highest mountain in the world outside of Asia, second tallest of the "seven summits," and seventeenth highest peak in the world.

Aconcagua is massive and tall, and while it is in a fairly gentle latitude compared to, say, Denali in Alaska, as you climb higher you enter a region where the air is cold and thin and where storms breed. The winds blow ferociously and the temperatures drop far below freezing. Frostbite and hypothermia are common in climbers who are improperly equipped, caught unprepared, or just unlucky. Those are routine risks in high-altitude climbing. Others include cerebral and pulmonary edema—excessive fluid buildup and retention around, respectively, the brain or the lungs—both of which can be fatal. The symptoms of these conditions can be missed by climbers because of a condition called "hypoxia," brought on by the anemic air. Along with lethargy, headaches, and other symptoms, breathing insufficient oxygen results in poor judgment. Climbers get in trouble because they shrug off the warning signs of, say, a cerebral edema.

While all this is part of high-altitude climbing, there is a lot more to it. The exhilaration is easily worth the pain. I had believed that, anyway, during the months I had been training and preparing for this climb. And I had looked forward to this day, when I would be starting out on this trail, this climb—say it, this *adventure*—with my daughter as keenly as I could remember anticipating anything in my life. It seemed like a long time now that we had been talking about this day, first by phone and e-mail, and then face-to-face on the plane down from JFK, through Miami, and on to Santiago. This was our big climb. We had trained for it and we were in good shape. I felt eager and confident and also sweetly fortunate to be here, doing this with my daughter. Felt it right up until we started down the trail and were met by the beaten man on the back of that mule. Then the doubts that I had managed to keep suppressed rose up and seized me by the throat.

What have I gotten us into?

The question took me back several years, to when I first visualized myself climbing mountains. Back then I had imagined myself doing it alone, and I wondered now whether my mistake was in dreaming of climbing in the first place or, perhaps, in bringing my daughter into the picture and, eventually, both of us here.

Since it is impossible to know the future, I recalled the past as I made my way along the trail. The answer to the question *What have I gotten us into?* would be clear soon enough. In the meantime, I could amuse myself by remembering how we had gotten here. It was, after all, one of my better memories.

The Seed of Obsession

There I beheld the emblem of a mind
That feed upon infinity
                    —Wordsworth

The mountain was clear and distinct, from the river where I was fishing, fifty miles away. It rose angular and dramatic out of the flat plains country, with no foothills to soften its impact, and even when the fishing was good, I had a hard time taking my eyes off it. There was something irresistible about it, something compelling that seemed to demand my attention.

Part of the mountain's appeal, I realized, was sheer unfamiliarity and novelty. I was a citizen of the lowlands and had spent virtually my entire life, until my thirties, at sea level. I considered the Gulf coast around the Alabama-Florida line my childhood home (my father was Navy, so we moved a lot) and the highest "peak" in that area was a clay bluff, elevation some 300 feet. I was a fairly adventuresome boy but climbing, understandably, did not figure into my calculations. As an adult, I had lived in Chicago, then New York before I married my wife and we moved to Vermont to raise a family.

Vermont, of course, is the "Green Mountain State," and after a decade or so of living there, I still found the views seductive.

I especially enjoyed watching the sunsets and the way the colors played off a mountain I could see through the picture window of my living room. That "mountain," however, was a little over 3,000 feet high. I hiked and skied up its slopes and those of a sister peak that, at almost 4,000 feet, is as tall as mountains get in Vermont.

The Green and Taconic mountains are old and round, smoothed to gentle domes by the winds of geologic time until you can ride a bicycle up and down their slopes, provided you can find an old logging trail, which isn't difficult. Most of these mountains were cleared for timber and to make pastures. They have grown back in this century, but they are still exceedingly manageable mountains. Nothing more than well-worn hills, really.

So the view of the Tetons—and especially the Grand Teton—was novel and arresting to me as I waded the Henry's Fork of the Snake River. I might have been the country boy who sets eyes for the first time on the skyline of Manhattan and swears that someday this will be his domain. Except I wasn't quite there yet or, if I was, I didn't realize it. I was just looking, but I was enchanted. The looming silhouette of the Grand Teton, with its signature crook, put there by exposure to the wind, spoke to something in me, even if I didn't understand the language.

▲ ▲ ▲

A few days later I was in Jackson, Wyoming. My first view of the Tetons had been from Idaho, looking east. Jackson lies virtually in the (afternoon) shadow of the mountains, on the east side. Jackson Hole was where the early mountain men of the John Colter, Jim Bridger, Jeremiah Johnson era came to trade and raise hell once a year in what they called "rendez vous." In the twentieth century, Jackson had become a tourist town and a fairly shabby one at that, until John D. Rockefeller Jr. decided the area was so stunningly beautiful it required protection from the pressures of commerce. He bought up much of the land, and eventually it was acquired by the government. Now the Tetons themselves are part of a national park adjacent to the more famous Yellowstone. Much of the surrounding land is national forest. The town of Jackson is still something of a vulgar tourist trap, but the region is spectacular enough that it cannot be spoiled by the existence of the Cowboy Bar and a Ralph Lauren outlet. People come to Jackson and the Tetons for all kinds of outdoor sport. There is whitewater rafting on the Snake River. Climbing in the mountains. Horseback riding at a number of dude ranches. Fishing on Flat Creek. Skiing in the winter. Successful people with a taste for the outdoors live in expensive homes outside of town.

When I made my visit to Jackson, I was a magazine journalist researching an article about environmental issues. Conservationists were trying to keep oil exploration out of one of the Forest Service parcels, and the fight had ramifications for the entire West.

I went around town for three or four days, interviewing environmentalists, geologists, developers, and concerned observers, all of whom I found interesting enough, but not as interesting as the mountain. If I could catch a glimpse of the Grand through the window of someone's office, first my eyes and then my attention would go there. I would continue taking notes and asking the follow-up questions, but my mind and my focus would be on the mountain.

From this side, and this close, the Grand cast a different sort of spell. From fifty miles away, where I'd been fishing, it looked like it could have been painted by a delicate watercolorist on the blue canvas of the horizon. Up close, it was something else entirely: simultaneously brutal and austere, a product of immense forces, geological or divine or both, but certainly not the work of some delicate pointillist.

One morning, during an interview with a woman who knew the area, I asked if many people climbed that mountain.

"Oh, yes," she said. "Dozens of them."

Was there a place where they started, I asked, a trailhead or something? I wanted a closer look at the mountain and, maybe, a word or two with someone who had climbed it. While mountains were unfamiliar, even exotic, to me, I had read a lot of the climbing literature. I was an admirer of Walter Bonatti, Willi Unsold, Jim Whittaker, and of course, Edmund Hillary. I could remember reading, nonstop, the account of the first summit of Everest in the *National Geographic* at my grandparents' home in Atmore, Alabama. I'd never seen a mountain back then and didn't expect I ever would.

"Up by Jenny Lake," the woman said. "There's a guide service called Exum."

That afternoon, I drove north up the Snake River valley to Moose, which was not much more than a post office and general store sharing the same building. Off the main road, I found a small hut that belonged to Exum, oldest mountain guide service in America and employer of some of the most accomplished climbers in the world.

Climbing ropes and harnesses hung from pegs on the walls of the shed. Packs had been left lying in corners. A young woman sitting behind a desk asked if she could help me.

"I, uh, was just wondering if you send climbers out of here."

"We sure do," she said cheerfully.

"To climb the big mountain?"

"The Grand," she said. "Yes. It's one of our most popular climbs."

"How much experience do you need?" I asked, thinking years.

"How much climbing have you done?" she asked. There was a note of kindness in her voice.

"None," I said.

"Well," she said, "if you want to climb the Grand, you'll have to go to our two-day climbing school first."

Two days.

"That's all?"

She smiled. "It's a very thorough school. The guides who teach it are the best."

"Only two days?"

"Yes."

"Then what?"

"Then, if you still want to climb the Grand, you sign up for a climb. It takes two days."

Two days.

"You mean I could do the whole thing in less than a week?"

She smiled. "Some people do. Most people put some time between the school and the climb. And you don't want to schedule yourself too tightly, because you can always run into problems with the weather."

I stood there for a moment, looking at the coiled climbing ropes and the other gear hanging from the pegs on the walls, and thinking that if I really wanted to do this thing, I could call home and say I was staying for an extra week. Two days for the school and two days for the climb. It was very tempting.

"Would you like to sign up for the school?"

"Can I get back to you?"

"Sure."

She gave me a brochure and I thanked her. On the highway back to Jackson, my eyes kept leaving the road and staring up at the Grand.

I studied the brochure when I got back to my motel and was surprised at the cost of the school and the climb. It seemed low, just a little more than what I had recently paid for a guided float trip down the Madison River. I considered calling the woman at the Exum hut and telling her to sign me up for the next two-day school and then a climb of the big mountain. But I went shopping, instead, and then packed, asked for an early wake-up call, and in the morning, flew out of Jackson for Albany, New York, and home. I planned to climb the Grand, but some other time.

Girls Are Great for the Dad

The lucky man has a daughter as his first child.
—Spanish proverb

My daughters were waiting up past their bedtimes to see me when I got home, and they greeted me at the door, where I picked them up, one in each arm, and they hugged my neck with their little arms and kissed my cheeks. Brooke, the older, was four. Her younger sister, Hadley, was not quite two. After I put them down, I gave them the turquoise and silver jewelry I had bought the day before in Jackson, and they thanked me lavishly and hugged me again. They were happy with their presents, but they were also happy to have me home. There wasn't anything fake about the way they sat in my lap and told me excitedly about what they had been doing while I was gone. The dog, Abe, had gotten into a skunk. Mom had taken them someplace to eat ice cream. They'd cooked out on the grill and had a picnic. I listened and I told them about what I'd been doing, and then I took them up to their room and read to each of them from their favorite books and said their prayers with them before I turned out the light, gave them each a kiss, and said good night.

"They really missed you," my wife, Marsha, said later, when we were sitting in the living room, talking and catching up. I'd been gone almost two weeks.

"Well, I missed them, too," I said. "Missed them a lot." I said it as though this was, somehow, mystifying to me. Which, in truth, it was. Fatherhood was a mysterious state and didn't seem to become any less so with time and familiarity. At night, when I looked in on my sleeping daughters, I would feel a deep sense of improbability mingled with inadequacy.

"Well, they love their dad," my wife said, smiling. "They talked about you the whole time you were gone, and they asked me every morning if you were coming home today. Must be nice to be so adored."

"It is," I said. "But I don't know what I did to deserve it."

"You didn't do anything," she said. "Little girls are just that way about their daddies."

This seemed undeniably true. I didn't have to do much, if anything, to rate a hug from one of my girls. They liked to bring me the pictures they had drawn and the little bouquets of wildflowers—Queen Anne's lace, Indian paintbrushes, black-eyed Susans, and the like—that they had carefully picked in the meadow behind the house. They liked for me to read to them. When Hadley was being difficult about eating, the solution was easy—I'd feed her. She would always eat for me. With Marsha, it was sometimes yes and sometimes emphatically no.

The word to describe my initial attitude toward fatherhood is, I suppose, "indifferent." Somewhere in my reading I had come across a line that struck me as the right approach: "The greatest gift a man can give his children is to love their mother." I put that line into my journal before Brooke was born and figured that would be the star by which I'd navigate. Fathers have duties and mothers have instincts. I made up my mind not to be an aloof, absentee father. Not because I felt some blood-deep urge to nurture but because my wife wanted it to be that way.

▲ ▲ ▲

Before I married I had spent most of my time in the company of men. It was where I felt comfortable. I liked life in the barracks (I'd been in the Army), the saloons, the hunting and fishing camps. I believed it was time, once I became a husband and father, to put all that behind me, and in fact, it wasn't hard and I didn't often miss the old things. Sometimes, when the kids were being especially difficult and it seemed like I could not escape the sound of an infant's crying, but not often.

But while I did not miss the old life, I felt unqualified for the new one. I was an old-fashioned man, unable or unwilling to change with the times. There had been a movement in the culture, spawned by the successes of feminism, for men to become sensitive and get in touch with their feelings. I didn't even try. Nor, later on, did I attend campfires where men beat on tom-toms and chanted in order to cultivate their primitive natures.

I knew it wouldn't work and that I would have to get by with the material at hand. I resolved, over and over, to do the best I could with what I had—an old male oath—and that is what I did. And, of course, I never once felt up to the job.

This would have also been true, I suppose, if I'd had sons. But I felt especially inadequate as the father of girls. For now, being a father was enough. More than enough, actually, and being the father of girls made it even more challenging. I didn't have any idea of what I was supposed to do or how to do it right. With boys, I could have at least fallen back on memories of the times I spent with my own father. There had been long separations when he was at sea, but when he was home, we'd gone on fishing trips together and those times had been important, the way they are for boys. I worked hard to live up to what I thought of as my father's expectations. When it was my father's turn to fish, I would take the stern and paddle the boat while he sat in the bow, casting methodically to likely looking spots along the bank. The idea was to keep him just the right distance off the bank, at optimum casting distance. When I did it, he would tell me I'd done a good job and I would swell with pride. When he told me to pay attention to what I was doing and get him closer, or farther away, I would feel like I had let him down. He was a big man, a naval officer and a pilot, and he had an air of easy authority. He seldom raised his voice when I did something wrong on one of those fishing trips, but then, he didn't have to.

It wouldn't have been easy, necessarily, if I'd had sons, but it might have been easier. I would have had a model to follow. I could have taken them on fishing, camping, and canoeing trips. I was an outdoorsman and made my living writing about fishing, hunting, scuba diving, and the like. The column I wrote for *Esquire* magazine was called "Outdoors," and had been described in the press as "macho," which was a word I did not like much but could not seem to avoid.

I said something, once, about how ill equipped I felt when it came to raising girls, to my brother who was the father of two boys.

He put his hand on my shoulder and said, "Well, bro, I don't know what to tell you, but one thing is for sure."

"What's that?"

"You can't throw them back."

▲ ▲ ▲

If I didn't have any very firm ideas about how to be a good father to daughters, I had plenty of negative examples. The literature of feminism was full of uncaring, unfeeling, absentee fathers whose daughters had suffered from their neglect or their outright abuse. The remote, unempathetic dad was pretty much a stock character of the times, and you were never surprised when you heard a grown woman say that she hated her father, even if he'd never done anything worse than forget her birthday.

Fathers at the time were generally depicted as patriarchal bastards who did not know their own children in any intimate sense. Men cared more about their careers and their cronies than they did about their families. They were indifferent, at best—violent, at worst. Fathers—especially traditional fathers—were increasingly thought of as unnecessary to the successful raising of children. There was a nascent movement for a new, nurturing sort of father, the kind who was deeply involved with the raising of his children, and there were men around who could change a diaper as adroitly as they could change a tire. But in spite of movies like *Kramer vs. Kramer,* the trend did not seem to have real legs. Most men wanted to be good fathers and assumed that this meant being good providers and occasional pals.

Truth was, I didn't know anything about being the kind of father who was "there" emotionally for his children, and I wasn't likely to learn much, either. I was empathy impaired and I knew it. But that probably wouldn't have made much difference if I'd had sons. I could have been a rule maker, example, and rival, and a little antagonism might not have been a bad thing. It had worked for a lot of men I knew.

But you want your daughters to adore you, the way my wife said they adored me, without reservation and without my doing anything to deserve it, for the sheer accidental reason that I was the only man in their young lives.

I had decided to give it my best, to try to be involved as a father even if it was something I did not feel with any instinctive urgency. I figured I would do it and, with luck, I would learn to like it. This was the old "fake it until you make it" strategy. So I learned how to change diapers and, in the case of Brooke, to spend hours holding her over my shoulder and walking around the room, bouncing softly on the balls of my feet until she got over the distress of colic and stopped crying. I got better at this than my wife and made sure she knew it. After each child graduated from breast feeding, I learned to fix them meals and, given the food, that was sometimes more of a trial than changing diapers.

One of my favorite jobs was giving them their baths at night, before bed, and then drying their fine baby hair and brushing it out with a soft brush. Brooke was very blonde and Hadley was very dark. One of many ways in which they were not just unalike, but opposites.

Brooke was serious and seemed to make everything she did into a project with objectives and goals. Hadley was spontaneous and a joker, and she went from one thing to another. When I read to them before bed, Brooke liked real stories with suspense and danger, conflict and resolution—*Peter Pan* was an early favorite. Hadley liked poems and stories about animals—*Ferdinand the Bull,* for instance—and stuff that was to me incomprehensible, like *Goodnight Moon.*

Observing these differences was fascinating. I liked answering Brooke's endless questions about why the sky was blue and so forth, and I liked watching Hadley play with the dog or the cat, operating on some intuitive sense of just how far she could go before she drove them away. After a while it occurred to me that I was often looking for opportunities to spend time with my daughters, not just doing what I thought I was required to do.

Without realizing it, I had become a fairly decent nurturing father. No credit to me, however, because this is what happens according to current research into the subject. "Males of the species," writes Sarah Blaffer Hrdy in her monumental study *Mother Nature,* "have it in them to be protective and nurturing of infants but the right triggers have to be present to elicit the desired responses." Darwin called these instincts "latent even in brain of male." Hrdy, who casts an exceedingly wide cultural net, finds examples in the George Eliot novel *Silas Marner* and the Tom Selleck film *Three Men and a Baby*. According to Hrdy's analysis, which cuts across the lines of cultural anthropology, evolutionary psychology, and several other fields, "Care is most readily elicited from a male primate under three conditions:

1. long-standing familiarity with the immature
2. the nearby infant is urgently in need of rescue, and, especially
3. the male has a relationship with the mother."

I was responding, then, to the old genetic codes and the evolutionary signals, which was fine even if it tends to make you feel a little less noble about your commitment to fatherhood. There is no equivalent work on fatherhood, by the way, to Hrdy's masterpiece on motherhood. But this is understandable; the one role is primary, instinctive, and at the absolute root of everything. The other is, well, a supporting role at best and pretty much what you make of it. I got lucky.

▲ ▲ ▲

Before my wife and I went off to bed, I looked in on my daughters to make sure they were warm and tucked in. Brooke was sleeping with a doll she called Carol. Hadley was clutching a ragged white baby blanket. They looked serene and untroubled and I watched them for a few minutes, feeling something thick at the center of my chest. Brooke was a very sound sleeper, but Hadley woke up at the smallest disturbance. When I reached into her crib to pull the covers up, her eyes came open with alarm. Then she saw my face, between her and the light, and she smiled and held up her arms for a hug.

At that moment, it seemed easy.

Competing for Attention

One father is more than a hundred schoolmasters.
— George Herbert

You don't realize it at the time but infancy, with the earaches and the toilet training and the crying in the night, is the easy part. Unless you let the television get the upper hand, you don't have any serious competition for your preschoolers' affections and attention. You are infallible, or close to it, in their eyes. This changes the first day they get on a school bus.

But before you begin the great struggle with the world of outside influences, you have to make some decisions yourself, even while your kids are infants. There is always a lot of free advice out there, and in the early 1980s, when my girls were in their preschool years, much of it insisted that there were no important, innate differences between boys and girls, that they learned gender roles and that if you gave girls dolls and boys tool sets, they would grow up learning to be, respectively, moms and mechanics. It was important, then, to let the children develop on their own and discover their own natures in an environment free of stereotyping.

The theory was avidly embraced by many parents, especially those (like me) who had girls and didn't want them growing up with limited expectations and dreams. Especially when they could turn on the television and see Sally Ride going into space. In the new regime, girls were not to be discouraged from playing ball and boys were supposed to get the message that dolls were okay. They would figure it out as individuals.

In the small Vermont town where we lived, there were not a lot of children. So few, that when it came to playmates, you didn't worry about gender. Brooke's favorite playmate was a boy who lived nearby and was a couple of months older. When he wasn't at our house, she was at his. This went on for several years. When the boy's sister came along, at roughly the time Hadley was born, the four of them became playmates.

In my little backyard laboratory, it became clear that there were differences. It was undeniable that the boy liked to throw balls more than the girls did. That he was less likely to obey the rules, more inclined to lose his temper, and not a natural when it came to cooperation. When we talked with other parents, this difference between boys and girls was a frequent topic. When some of our friends admitted that they had noticed the same thing, they sounded almost apologetic, as though they were being somehow subversive.

But if the boys in my backyard were more aggressive and active, the girls could be just as bold and tough. One afternoon, Brooke and the boy who was her playmate decided to climb a very tall pine tree on the edge of our yard. The tree had lots of strong limbs, well spaced for climbing, and I probably would have found it irresistible myself when I'd been their age. (Those who wonder why adults climb mountains should probably ask why children climb trees. The second question is, I suppose, an answer to the first.)

But . . . I was the grown-up now, and these were my kids— half of them, anyway. So sitting back in the shadows a little so they couldn't see me, I watched from my office window while they climbed the tree. They started out daring each other to go beyond the low limbs. The boy went a little higher and looked down at Brooke.

"Come on," he said. "Don't be a wimp." He picked up that kind of language from television.

"I'm not a wimp," said Brooke, who had been watching the same programs.

"Then, come on."

She climbed past him, up to where the branches were thin and bent under her weight. I watched a little nervously, wondering if I should go out and tell them to come down out of the tree. This was my little girl and I felt like I should protect her. But I kept quiet.

The boy climbed up to where Brooke was standing and then a little higher. He challenged her again. She climbed past him. They were 25 or 30 feet off the ground now, where the limbs were the thickness of broom handles. They were not saying anything, and I suspect they were both scared but neither was willing to quit. They moved another few feet up the tree, climbing very carefully, and I could feel my heart beating rapidly as I watched. If one of those limbs broke . . .

Finally, they worked out an arrangement. They would both climb another few feet, to a particular branch, and then they would both go down. Their voices sounded especially thin during these negotiations. They both seemed pleased with the settlement and I was thrilled. Also proud.

▲ ▲ ▲

In time, of course, the theory that there were no innate differences between boys and girls gave way to the conclusion that there were, indeed, differences and that they were deeply rooted and worth studying. The theoretical ground was broken by Dr. Edward O. Wilson, the Harvard biologist, who pioneered the theory of sociobiology, which took the insights of evolution into the realm of social behavior. His the-

ory that societies organized themselves, and individuals settled on roles within those societies, based on the principles of
natural selection was considered heretical when Wilson first
proposed it, and he was attacked vigorously in the journals
for the crime of validating gender roles and once had a pitcher
of water poured over his head when speaking in a public
forum.

With time, Wilson's insights spawned new scholarship and
new thinking, especially in the field of evolutionary psychology,
which attempted to account for human behavior as reflecting
strategies for insuring the survival of genes. In crude terms,
success in men followed from physical skills, aggression, and
the ability to find numerous mates and produce many offspring.
In women, from being able to attract strong mates and successfully rear relatively few offspring. Individuals with these
traits succeeded, in an evolutionary sense, and passed along
their genes over hundreds of generations. In the jargon of the
day, then, we are hardwired into our gender roles, and there is,
in fact, a biological basis for behavior. Eventually, the theory
was seen not as a validation of the inferiority, subservience,
and second-class status of women but, indeed, of their superiority, according to at least one evolutionary psychologist, Dr.
Helen Fisher of Rutgers. She argues in her book, *The First
Sex*, that the characteristics that are genetically hardwired
into women dictate their success in an increasingly complex
world that requires cooperation and web thinking, rather than
dominance and linear thinking.

All this was a long way from my backyard, where I did my
field research. I did, however, have occasion to interview Ed
Wilson for a magazine article and found him not merely bril-
liant (I expected that) but also a warm and genial man with a
lively sense of humor. We talked at his Harvard office, where
colonies of ants in terrariums went about their business. It
turned out that Wilson had also grown up on the Gulf coast of

Alabama and Florida and that he and I had prowled some of the same swamps and beaches.

Wilson was a man you could admire as much for his civility as his brilliance. Civility was a rare thing in the general conversation about gender roles, motherhood, fatherhood, and such matters. Frequently, the discussion got down to the level of "my gender is better than your gender," or to a kind of tired, ideological orthodoxy that always seemed so far from the real business of being a parent—father or mother. You could read, for instance, an article in the *American Psychologist* called "Deconstructing the Essential Father," which claimed dads weren't all that necessary, there wasn't much evidence that fatherhood civilized men or provided protection for children, and men could be "detrimental" to mothers and their children.

Which wasn't much help if you were trying to be a father. The models provided by the popular culture weren't any better. If you couldn't aim any higher than Homer Simpson, then what was the point?

As my girls got older, the dynamic changed. I wasn't giving them baths and reading them stories before bed any longer. But I was still their dad and I still wanted to be involved.

I couldn't be a role model even if I tried, and anyway, they had their mother for that. Marsha had, typically, decided that when she became a mother, she would do it full-out, full-time. She was a resourceful, independent woman before we met, and that hadn't changed in any fundamental way. She had been one of the first women reporters at *Forbes* magazine, produced and directed commercial films, worked as a professional photographer, and been a partner in a New York graphics firm. Among other things.

Now, by choice, she was the full-time mother of two girls. If they needed someone they wanted to grow up and be like, they had her, which was as it should be and as I wanted it.

Marsha threw herself into the raising of her girls. She or-

ganized play groups, taught them to ski (and learned herself),
taught Sunday school, found plays and concerts, and then
drove, sometimes a hundred miles, to expose her daughters to
the things they were missing by living in Vermont. She was
also a tall, striking woman who knew how to cook and could
knit sweaters and smock dresses. She was all the role model
our daughters needed.

My role, then, was to be a provider and a dad. Which came
down to being something that really has no other name. I was
not exactly a companion or a pal, but still, something of that.
Nor was I simply a distant, slightly scary authority figure;
though, again, that was part of it. And I wasn't just the guy
who was here and gone, who paid the bills and worried about
money even if there were times when I felt like that pretty
much described it and, probably, so did they.

As the girls got older and, especially, when they started
school, it became clearer to me what my duties as dad were.

▲ ▲ ▲

Marsha and I had thought, naively, that when we moved to
Vermont we had escaped from the temptations of drugs, alcohol, easy sex, early dropout, and general ruin that is pretty
much a part of growing up in modern America. But we learned.
Not long after we had established ourselves in Vermont, a high
school kid in town was killed when he left a party, lay down in
a road, and was run over by another kid who did not stop. He
later told the police that he thought he'd hit a deer. Stories
about that party, and others, made it pretty clear that moving
to the country was not the answer. You could run, but you could
not hide. MTV would find you.

When our girls went up to the local elementary school, their
playmates included one girl whose mother went to jail for dealing and another whose mom had a live-in boyfriend who was
known to beat her. That girl came to our house to play, and

when she was eight or nine years old, Marsha looked at her face with its forlorn, despairing eyes and general cringing expression of fear and said to me, "You know, she doesn't have a chance."

She was right. The girl eventually got a full scholarship to a prestigious prep school but was kicked out for using drugs. She came home, dropped out of high school, and by the time she was eighteen, was a single mother on both welfare and drugs. The girl whose mother did time got a similar scholarship and was also expelled from school for drug use. She never finished school and wound up waiting tables.

As a way to hold on to our girls, Marsha and I made an effort to find things we could all do together, things that would divert them, at least temporarily, from the temptations of their peers. It is, oddly, one of the toughest challenges families face. In a world where everyone seems to have so little time, families can't seem to find anything to do together even when they have a breather. More and more, family time is a trip to the mall. Or a vacation in Las Vegas.

Which struck me as sad. We made up our minds to resist that, and if any one act or decision could be said to account for why I wound up, with Brooke, on the face of Aconcagua, then that was it.

▲ ▲ ▲

Like all Vermont kids, my daughters learned to ski at a very early age and skiing was something we could do together, as a family. I had never skied before we moved to Vermont. Neither had Marsha, but we both learned. I turned out to be the least accomplished skier in the group, couldn't keep up with my own kids. But we weren't in competition. It might have been different, I suspected, if they'd been boys.

Still, Brooke and Hadley were bold skiers and they took chances, which I encouraged. I liked watching them, usually from behind, as they stood on the edges of their skis—and later, their snowboards—or grabbed some air. Brooke broke an arm when she was learning on the board, and Hadley took what she called an eggbeater that resulted in a concussion and a trip to the hospital for a CAT scan to make sure she didn't have a hematoma or a fractured skull. She never did remember the fall and kept asking her friends to describe it. But the injuries didn't slow them down or make them more cautious.

Marsha and I liked that. We were happier to have them on the ski mountains, taking those chances, than to have them in town, where the risks were different and a lot harder to manage. Broken bones and concussions began to seem like healthy alternatives to drugs and dropping out. If it was an either/or proposition, then I would wish broken bones on my kids. That kind of thinking, no doubt, led straight to Aconcagua.

It also played into what I knew I could do as a father. If I couldn't "be there" for them emotionally, as an empathetic dad, then I would be there *with* them, when we went camping, canoeing, skiing or, even, scuba diving, together on a couple of trips to a little bare-bones resort in the Bahamas.

It was a good life, especially for me. Girls, as many people have said, are great for the dad. I was neither rival nor role model when we were doing these things but some sort of combination coach and companion. I liked it because it meant I got to watch my girls grow up and become who they were, and they were two very different people. Brooke was good in school and something of a loner. She was not very good in sports—the proverbial last kid chosen and the one who spent most of her time on the sidelines—and this made her more lonely and stoic. She became a reader and spent a lot of time with books. Hadley, on the other hand, had lots of trouble with school (we found out, eventually, that she had a learning disability) but was gregarious, extroverted, and very popular. While she wasn't much better at sports than Brooke, she was always included.

I learned these things and tried to provide whatever comfort and encouragement I could. And I found I liked being involved in their lives. I went on Hadley's eighth-grade class trip to Montreal as a chaperon. Half a dozen mothers and me. My job was to speak sternly to the boys when they got out of hand on the bus or in the hotel.

I also coached a girls softball team in a local league. I started as a volunteer assistant to the head coach the first year Brooke played. I didn't know anything about coaching and Brooke didn't know anything about playing softball. She sat on the bench a lot and I studied the man who coached the team. He was a fine athlete and actually an assistant football coach at Williams College, which had one of the best teams in the country among small elite schools. This man knew what he was doing, and I learned a lot from him and a little from a couple of books I read. His daughter was the star of the team, but it was her last year of eligibility. After she was too old to play, her father was no longer interested in coaching. So I inherited the Wonder Women and remained as head coach and bus driver for seven years, until Hadley had used up her last year of eligibility.

They were good years. I was traveling a lot, making my living as a magazine writer, but during the season I could usually work the schedule around so I'd be home for games and practices. I made it just in time for a few games, straight from the Amtrak station, still wearing a necktie. I got to know the girls on the team and, inevitably, their stories. Whose parents were breaking up and that sort of thing. When a girl was having that kind of trouble, it showed and I had no idea how to handle it except to hit a few extra grounders her way and say, "Attagirl," with a little extra enthusiasm when she fielded one cleanly and made a good throw to first. My reaction, then, to serious emotional storms—and there were a lot of them—was to coach a little harder. If you could get a girl's attention, then for two hours of practice or a game, anyway, she could think about something other than what was hurting her. She could concentrate on keeping her eye on the ball and her mind in the game (my mantra) so that we could beat the hated Peaches.

Coaching gave me a chance to work a little with Brooke, who was not as fast or as coordinated as some of the other girls. But she was determined. So I put her at first base, where she didn't have to range very far to make plays and told her that her job was to catch, or stop, every ball that was thrown to her by one of the other infielders. We worked on watching the ball all the way into the glove and on positioning herself so that if she did bobble the throw, she could block the ball with her body. Other girls would flinch and turn away from a ball that was in the dirt. I told her that even if the ball short hopped and hit her in the face, the worst would be a bloody nose.

"You can handle that, right?"

"Right," she said.

She caught a couple with her face but always picked the ball up in time to force the out.

I'm not sure I was a very good coach—certainly not in my predecessor's league—but I know I worked hard at it because it didn't seem like work. And I think the girls felt a certain kind of regard for me, though my daughters tell me I was something of an enigma to most of my players. Brooke and Hadley can still get each other laughing, almost hysterically, by recalling the day when I was instructing the Wonder Women on how I thought they should run out every ball they hit, even the fouls.

"Now, what I want you to do," Brooke or Hadley will say, doing her imitation of old Dad, "is when you get some wood on that ball, don't stand there admiring it. What you do is, you put your head down and you run like a scalded dog in the direction of first base."

At this point, whoever is telling the story, shifts to the role of a bewildered ten-year-old Vermont girl trying to figure out what this madman who sounds vaguely like someone found him on the *Andy Griffith Show* means. How *does* a scalded dog run, anyway, and what kind of person goes around scalding dogs? Very strange behavior in a coach.

Well, it was fun for me. More than fun. And I suppose I got a lot more out of it than any of the girls I coached. It goes that way with fatherhood.

I liked teaching/coaching so much that I got even further in over my head by agreeing to teach Sunday school at the Congregational church in our town. I was far less qualified to teach Sunday school than I was to coach softball. I had no theological training and I certainly had not led a life of rectitude. I was asked only because I'd been one of those parents who drops the kids off every Sunday, hoping that something will rub off and they will, eventually, make up their own minds about all of that stuff.

But I was asked and I said yes, probably because coaching softball had been so satisfying and I thought there might be a measure of the same kind of satisfaction in teaching Sunday school. Brooke would be in my class, and then Hadley. For a couple of years, if I lasted that long, I would have both of them. That counted for a lot.

I had no idea what to teach and the material I was given—a lot of glorified comic books with some tepid messages, mostly about tolerance—didn't excite me and I couldn't imagine it would stimulate the kids. So I found a book that told the durable Bible stories in language suitable for kids, and every Sunday morning, I would sit around a table with several kids— anywhere from three to ten—and we would read those stories and talk about them.

I had thought that the simplest, most straight-ahead stories would be the most appealing to my group. Give them David and Goliath and Noah and the Ark and treat it like Disney material, was my thought. But I was underestimating my students. To my vast surprise, the stories that seemed to genuinely engage them were the dark, awesome, paradoxical stories that have challenged the greatest theological minds in the world—Abraham and Isaac and, especially, Job.

We spent weeks, every year, on Job. I would ask my pupils this question: "How, if God is all-merciful, do we account for suffering in this world?" And then we would read Job and talk about it. And the kids, of course, would say things that were dazzlingly insightful. One Sunday morning, slightly hungover, I sat at the head of the table and listened to an 11-year-old explain to me that suffering was a gift from God, just like any challenge is really a gift. The parents of one of my kids called me and told me that their daughter had come home from my Sunday school class and told them what I'd been teaching.

"She seems very interested in the class," I said noncommittally. I was braced for a storm. How could I teach this depressing, downer stuff to kids . . . and so forth.

"You know what she said?" the mother asked me.

"Uh, no."

"She said that when she dies she wants the words on her tombstone to be something from your class about, 'Naked came I into the world . . .' "

" 'And naked shall I return,' " I said, finishing the verse for her when she stumbled, " 'The Lord giveth and the Lord taketh away. Blessed be the name of the Lord.' "

"That's it," the woman said. "I thought it was kind of cute and that you'd like to know."

I did. And I thanked her.

On another occasion, a parent called to tell me that she'd come in a little early to pick up her child from another class, and as she stood outside the door of the room where I was teaching, she could hear the sound of a single voice—mine—but could not make out the words. After a while there would be a pause, followed by a chorus of 10- to 12-year-old voices, saying in unison, "Suffering, suffering."

"What exactly are you teaching?" the woman said a little nervously. Her daughter would be in my class in a year or two.

"Oh," I said, "I just asked them to tell me the theme of the book of Job."

"I see."

We studied some more upbeat material, especially the sermon on the mount and the beatitudes, and I remember one of the girls in my class reciting, during a reading to the entire adult congregation, the lines about "Lay not up for yourselves treasures on earth where moths and rust doth corrupt and thieves break in and steal . . ." and listening apprehensively with the rest of my students because this girl, who had a lisp, had mangled the lines, over and over, in rehearsal, saying, "Steves break in and thiel."

But she got it right in church and we all applauded silently. In our class, those lines were some of our favorites. We talked about them a lot. I remember feeling awfully puny, sitting at a table with a handful of kids, talking about how the poor were blessed for they would inherit the kingdom of heaven. We were in a little room with a blackboard and we all had Bibles. I had the book of Bible stories written for young adults. It seemed pretty meager when you considered that these kids were part of a culture that included MTV and Nintendo games. I felt severely outgunned and this was before the internet explosion. My kids were attentive for the hour that I had them and that is testimony, I suppose, to the durability of those biblical stories.

Eventually, Sunday school, like softball, came to an end and it seemed like there was less and less that I could teach anyone, especially my own daughters. I found myself increasingly playing the role of some sort of present-day Polonius, giving a lot of pompous advice when, for instance, Brooke went off to boarding school. Giving advice is, I suppose, a fatherly sort of thing to do, but it is a lot less satisfying than teaching. It was around then that I decided to resurrect my plan to climb the Grand.

Let's Do This Together

Oh the mind, mind has mountains; cliffs of fall
Frightful, sheer, no-man-fathomed.
                    —Gerard Manley Hopkins

Y ou know what I'm going to do for my birthday," I said at
dinner one night.

"What's that?" Marsha, my wife, said.

"Climb a mountain." This was the first I'd ever brought my
plan out into the open.

"Any particular mountain?"

"The Grand Teton," I said. "In Wyoming."

"I want to go, too," Brooke said. She was fifteen, home from
school for a few days.

I shook my head.

"Why not?" she said.

I didn't have a good answer. But I wasn't singling her out.
I didn't want anyone coming along. It might have been the
lingering influence of some of the reading I'd done. Most of
the literature of climbing made it a solitary calling. Walter
Bonatti, the great Italian climber whose account of his winter ascent of the North Face of the Matterhorn had impressed me deeply, was the outstanding example of this kind
of climber. He went into the mountains like a lonely, melan-

choly penitent, seeking to rescue his soul or perish in the attempt.

"I want to make this trip alone," I said.

It was the wrong thing to say. A stupid thing to say. I realized that as soon as I saw the wounded look on my daughter's face.

Hadley looked at her plate. Marsha frowned. Brooke's eyes filmed over.

"I'm not talking about an afternoon hike," I said. "This is a serious mountain. People get hurt. Even die." (I didn't know this for sure, but it seemed like a reasonable guess.)

Nobody said anything.

"You use ropes and pitons," I said. "And you have to go to a training school first. It is the real thing." Actually, it had been a long time since anyone had hammered pitons into the face of the Grand. These days, climbers used hardware they could remove.

"So?" Marsha said, but I dug in my heels. I had been nursing the dream of climbing that mountain for a long time now. My fiftieth birthday seemed like a perfect time. Richly symbolic . . . or something.

I looked at my plate for a while, then said, "Maybe another time. But I'm going to do this one alone."

We finished dinner and did the dishes in cold silence. And nobody had much to say to me for the rest of the night. Certainly, nobody tried to change my mind, and I was determined not to let it happen.

But I thought about it that night, in the dark, when I couldn't sleep. Brooke had been away at school for four or five months, and I'd missed her, which was predictable. But in the few days that she had been home, I realized, I still missed her. She was slipping away from me and it seemed too soon for that. Also, she was having a tough time at boarding school. It was one of those old Eastern places, and most of the kids came from socially well-connected and affluent families in places like Greenwich, Connecticut. Brooke was a country mouse among them and had been snubbed enough by girls her age who were used to doing their own shopping at Tiffany's that she had withdrawn. And the school put a heavy emphasis on sports. She ran cross-country and finished all her races, but she was slowest on her team. Alone and unhappy, she had channeled all her considerable will and determination into academics. She was honor roll but this, perversely, further isolated her and cut her off from the cool kids.

I had tried talking to her but it didn't help. She'd merely said that she'd be all right. She wasn't quitting. While we had always been able to talk, these conversations were forced and abrupt. She would answer my questions by saying yes, no, or not really. And when she wanted to cut it off, she would say, "Dad, it's okay. Really."

I wasn't fool enough to think I could guide her through the storms of adolescence, but I thought that maybe it would be some kind of relief for her to spend a little time with the family, doing something, like we used to do. It would be good for me; I was sure of that.

As for the notion of the solitary climb to celebrate my fiftieth birthday, that was narcissistic, self-indulgent crap. My father had never made it this far, having died of cancer at 49. I'm sure that given the choice of spending his fiftieth with his two young daughters or seeking solitary epiphanies, he wouldn't have hesitated.

The only thing that could be better, I thought, than climbing the Grand with Brooke would be to climb it with the entire family. I began to see that picture in my mind, with the clarity that comes at two a.m., and think, "Why not?"

I brought it up at dinner that night.

"I think we should all go. Seriously."

"Not me," Marsha said. "Not in this lifetime."

"Why not?"

"I don't like heights. I'd be afraid of falling."

"You won't fall. There's almost no chance of that."

"And I know how to be absolutely certain."

I couldn't change her mind. Nor Hadley's. She did not like the idea of falling, either. Hadley had always been more careful and less impulsive than Brooke. And she didn't need to climb some mountain to test herself; she was challenged every day, at school, by a learning disability and the taunts of kids who laughed at her in class when she had trouble reading the words on the blackboard. She would come home crying, often, and I would try in my clumsy, helpless way to reassure her that she was not stupid, that she just had a different way of learning. My wife had the same conversation with Hadley and was much better at it, much more convincing. I ached for her when I tried to help her with her schoolwork and saw the way she struggled. When you are a parent, you are willing to do anything. The problem is that there often isn't much you can do. I told Hadley that it would get better for her, that life for her would begin after high school. But that was a long, long way off.

So I tried to persuade her to come to mountain climbing school with Brooke and me.

"No timed or written tests," I said.

She scowled at that bad joke. She has a lovely, mobile face that radiates pleasure or displeasure, whichever the case. I always knew exactly how Hadley felt about things, and it was clear she didn't like being teased on that point.

I was having a bad time of it at the dinner table these days.

"Well," I said to Brooke, "then it's just you and me."

"No, Dad. You go."

I tried but could not persuade her. She was firm, so I dropped it.

Later, after we had eaten and done the dishes, I talked to Brooke alone. I started out by apologizing again.

"That's okay," she said. "It's your deal. I shouldn't have barged in."

"I didn't have any idea you'd want to go along," I said. "You caught me by surprise."

She nodded.

"I think it would be great to do it together," I said.

"No, Dad, I understand . . ."

We went back and forth and I started to get a little irritated, thinking that she was making me pay a pretty heavy price for my blunder. But then I recognized something in her expression and her tone. She was being generous, trying to do something nice for her dad. I recognized it because I had seen it before.

I said, "Come on. We'll do it together." And I gave her a hug. "Please."

"You're sure?"

"Absolutely."

"Okay," she said.

And I was thrilled. Just like that, my plan of ten years had changed entirely. Where I had seen myself making my solitary way up the mountain toward the summit and some other, ineluctable thing that I could approach only alone, the vision now included my daughter. There was something of the quest in that original vision, something almost sacramental. When I thought back to the way my eyes had been drawn to the mountain during that visit to Jackson, my mind involuntarily recalled scripture:

> *I will life up mine eyes unto the hills*
> *From whence cometh my strength.*

Now I imagined myself making my way toward the summit, roped to my daughter, the two of us singing the Monty Python ditty that was sort of a family song on long car trips or when we were riding the ski lift together:

Oh, I'm a lumberjack and I'm okay
I sleep all night and I work all day.
I cut down trees, I eat my lunch.
And have buttered scones with tea.

The more I thought about it, the more I liked it. The only thing better would have been all four of us doing it together, like in the old days of family camping trips and cross-country skiing expeditions. But that was not going to be. So I would take what I could get.

The Risks Are Real

Give me health and a day and I will make the pomp of emperors ridiculous.   —Emerson

We flew into Jackson in late August. All four of us. I had decided, after the dinner conversation and my talk with Brooke, that even if Marsha and Hadley did not want to climb, we could all make the trip west together. I made reservations for a week at a guest ranch in Big Sky and found a house in Jackson where we could stay while Brooke and I were in climbing school or on the mountain. Marsha and Hadley could drive up to Yellowstone or go rafting on the Snake River. There was plenty for them to do. It would be a nice family vacation.

When the pilot turned onto final, coming into Jackson, and lowered the wing on our side of the plane, the Tetons seemed to appear, suddenly, quite close and utterly majestic outside our window.

"Wow," Brooke said.

"Think you can handle the big one?" I said.

There was no question which one I was talking about. At 13,770 feet, the Grand is only a few hundred feet taller than Mt. Moran, the next highest of the Tetons. But it seems much larger, more massive and more formidable, unquestionably the dominant mountain in this lovely, isolated range. As we passed by, its eastern face seemed to be all hostile gray rock except for the deep white glacier that filled a cleft about halfway up. There was absolutely nothing soft in the mountain's aspect or profile.

"I don't know," Brooke said.

"What do you mean?"

"It just looks awfully big," she said. "Are you sure we can do it?"

"Absolutely," I said.

"You really think so?" Marsha said from the seat ahead of us. The mountain looked big to her, too, and I'm sure that first look had made her think apprehensively about sending her daughter up there. Any mother would think that way.

"Yes," I said. "It's actually an easy climb. And pretty safe, too."

"Sure, Dad," Hadley said. The youngest always gets to be the wise guy.

"Really," I said.

"Then, why do you want to climb it?"

▲ ▲ ▲

We stayed in a ranch house on the banks of the Snake River in Moose, Wyoming. The house was ours by the kindness of a friend, and it was a beautiful, stately place with an unimpeded view of the Grand. We cooked out, the four of us, looking at the mountain and then the clear night sky, filling up with stars. We felt a long way from home and very close to one another. We built a fire of lodgepole logs in the big fireplace and stayed up late playing cards and laughing.

In the morning, Brooke and I reported to the Exum hut for the first day of climbing school. Marsha and Hadley drove on to Yellowstone.

The Exum hut was a busy place. In the time since I'd had my first thoughts about climbing mountains in general and

the Grand in particular, there had been an explosion of interest in all forms of outdoor recreation, including climbing. People in middle age who had never climbed before—like
me—were trying it, and not merely relatively modest mountains like the Grand but on the big ones, including the biggest
of all, Everest.

The first thing Brooke and I did, after introducing ourselves to a woman who was sitting behind a desk in the Exum
hut, was sign the routine releases. I looked the release over
without paying much attention. I didn't need to be told that
climbing was "inherently risky." It was the point. Like a lot of
middle-aged men, I seemed to spend most of my life sitting
down, and I often found myself thinking, fondly, of the first
time I jumped out of an airplane. I was ready for some risk and
willing to settle for merely a little movement. But what about
my daughter?

I had a moment, as I was reading over the boilerplate of the
release, when I realized with disturbing clarity that she could
get hurt, or worse, doing what we were getting ready to do. I
remembered an afternoon, a few years earlier, when she had
called me at the office I had rented so I could work away from
the house and asked if I knew where her mother was and when
she was coming home.

"I don't know, Brooke," I said. "What's the matter?"

"Nothing," she said. "I was just wondering." I could tell that
she was about to cry. She was ten. She wasn't supposed to call
me at the office unless it was an emergency.

"Brooke," I said sternly, "what's the matter?"

"It's nothing," she said. "I can wait for Mom."

I was, I suppose, fairly strict about the rules. If she had been
calling for some flimsy reason—because she wanted a ride to
some friend's house—I would have been hard on her. I was in
the middle of something and didn't want to be disturbed. But I
could tell this was serious.

"Come on," I said, trying to sound gentle. "You can tell me. I won't be upset."

"Really, Dad," she said, with her voice quaking, "it's no big deal."

"Brooke," I said. "Tell me what's wrong or I'll come home and find out for myself."

"I, uh, I think I broke my arm. But it isn't bad. I can wait till Mom gets home."

"I'll be right there," I said.

My office was only a few minutes from the house. She was waiting outside when I got there, bent over at the waist and cradling one arm with the other. She was clearly in pain. I felt a familiar stab of concern and guilt. Somehow, with your child, it is always your fault.

I helped her rig a sling and an ice bag for her arm. It was badly swollen, already turning blue at the most sensitive spot. It was plainly broken. I used a wet cloth to clean up her face, which was streaked with dirt and tears. Then I said, "Come on, I'll take you to the doctor."

"Dad, I can wait. Really. It's not that bad."

"Come on," I said. "We're going to the doctor. No arguments."

I tried to keep up a line of talk, to divert her, on the way to the doctor's office. And she tried to keep up her end, in spite of the pain. She was hustled right in for X rays, leaving me to fill out the insurance forms and flip the pages of the old magazines. I kept thinking about her. Ten years old and willing to endure a lot of pure physical pain for my sake.

I took her to the local Ben and Jerry's (a Vermont institution) after the doctor had put a cast on her arm. It would be there for six weeks. A fairly serious break. We ordered heath bar crunch and she told me how she had gone over the handlebars of her mountain bike on a trail not far from the house.

"I think I might have bent the wheel," she said.

"We'll fix it," I said.

"Can you?" she said, skeptically.

"If we can't, we'll get a new wheel. And if that doesn't work, we'll get a new bike."

▲ ▲ ▲

Brooke might have been 15, but in the Exum hut I saw a little blonde baby who seemed dangerously fragile. I wasn't sure I wanted her to sign that release.

"You sure you want to go through with this," I said before either of us had signed.

Brooke looked at me like she didn't understand the question.

"Sure," she said.

"Okay."

"Hey, Dad," she said, "don't tell me you're getting nervous."

"No."

"I mean, this was your idea."

"Right."

"Okay, then," she said, my baby girl now the picture of adolescent cockiness, "let's go for it."

We both signed, handed the releases to the woman behind the desk, then tried on helmets and harnesses, which we'd need once we started climbing.

Learning the Ropes

Perched with a rope around my waist, I saw the machinery of time.
                                                    —Robbin Fedden

Our teacher, on our first day of Exum's two-day course, was Al Read, one of the co-owners of Exum and probably the only person in the organization as old as I. While the other four people in our group were signing releases and organizing their equipment, I introduced myself. I knew from the brochure in the office (updated from the one that had been in my files for ten years) that he had been guiding for almost 25 years, since 1959 when he started with Exum, and that he had led climbs in the Himalayas. We were merely making small talk, but I studied him and paid attention to his words the way I would have if he'd been, say, a Formula One driver.

Read was not physically imposing, about my height and weight. But I was probably in better shape than he was. I'd been running and working out to get ready for the Grand. Read was a businessman/entrepreneur these days and spent most of his time behind a desk. But while he was, like me, physically unspectacular, there was something about Read that was arresting. It would be a stretch to call it an aura, but it was something and I didn't think I was imagining it.

He spoke softly and chose his words carefully, without wasted effort or emotion, and with the sort of composure you would expect from a big-stakes gambler or a test pilot.

Read did have one physical trait that was noticeable, even striking. His eyes. They were the kind of blue you see in ice sometimes—glacial ice, appropriately enough—and they were intense enough to make you slightly uncomfortable if you were talking to him and looking him in the eye.

I'd met one other serious mountain climber and he had the same kind of direct, intense eyes. That was Galen Rowell, one of the great American climbers and perhaps the greatest photographer of the high-altitude world. I'd spent a day in Yellowstone a few years earlier with Rowell, researching a story on him. There was the same composure in his manner that I found in Read, and I wondered if it was something common to all mountain climbers. It would make sense, I thought. Unnecessary moves would waste essential energy. Hasty or false moves would do worse than that. Efficiency would be a virtue.

"So," Read said, "you've never done any climbing before."

"Only ladders and trees," I said.

I expected him to use this opening by saying something encouraging like, "Don't worry, you'll do fine." But he merely nodded.

So I asked him, "Do most people who make it through the two-day course get to the top of the Grand?"

"Not really," he said in a not very reassuring way. Then, after what seemed like a long pause, he went on, "But a lot of people who go to the school aren't interested in the Grand in the first place. They just want to give rock climbing a try and see if they like it. Somebody might have it in the back of his mind that, 'Hey, I'll go for the big one if this course goes all right.' Then he finds out he doesn't like it and he doesn't come back after the first day."

"Why?"

Read shrugged. "Some people don't like heights."

"That's what my wife says. But she didn't sign up for the course."

"Just about everyone starts out here afraid of heights. It's only natural. Most people get over it when they learn to trust the techniques we teach them. But not everyone."

I had never considered the possibility that I might not like climbing or finish the school. I had simply assumed that I would go from the school to the top—the summit—of the Grand.

"What about the people who do finish the school and try the Grand?" I said. "How many of them make it?"

"I couldn't say exactly. The majority of them, certainly. But there are no guarantees."

This, I learned, is something that climbers feel non-climbers do not understand, so they make the point with special emphasis and in a number of ways. There are no guarantees in high-altitude climbing. You plan very carefully but you do not make predictions. You never know what might happen when you are on a mountain.

Some people can't handle the altitude, though the Grand isn't what you would call extreme altitude. But it is high enough to give some people problems. It isn't possible to predict how anyone will react to altitude. Sometimes, experienced climbers who have been at high altitude many times before will suddenly have problems.

As Read explained all this, I tried to remember if I had ever been higher than our present elevation, which was slightly over 6,000 feet. I was fairly sure I had not. I knew I hadn't ever been 13,000.

"Do a lot of people have problems that keep them from the summit?"

Read smiled a little. My apprehension was pretty obvious.

"Not a lot," he said. "But some."

And there was no way of knowing so it was pointless to worry about it.

"What else?" I said.

"You mean why do people not make it to the summit?"

I nodded.

"Weather is a big one. Weather is always unpredictable in the mountains. And a storm at altitude is a lot worse than the same storm in the valley. We had snow and 70-mile-an-hour winds up there just a couple of days ago."

It was a fine summer day. The air still had the morning coolness, the sky was clear and blue, and there was no wind.

"People go up there without the proper equipment—not in our groups, with our guides, but on their own—and the weather turns and they have to be rescued."

There was no point in worrying about the weather. It was, like my ability to adapt to altitude, a variable beyond my control. I was getting a feeling for why the two climbers I had met in my life both seemed so temperamentally serene. They operated in a universe of things they could control and things they could not. Knowing how to tell the difference was a survival skill. I was reminded of James Burnham's aphorism, one of my favorites: *Where there is no solution, there is no problem.*

I asked Read if some climbers did not make the summit because . . . well, because they *fell*.

"Exum has been here for more than 50 years," he said, "and we've had some accidents. We've had two fatalities that are what you would call recent. Both falls. One was a client who fell out of the harness in the climbing school area. We still don't know how that happened. Then another client fell on a climb. A guide told her to stay in one place and she moved. There have been a few injuries. Comes with the territory."

There was absolutely nothing defensive in the way Read said this, and he did not rush to reassure me with soothing words about how the chances of my falling and hurting myself while I was on the mountain were negligible, on a lower order of probability than my being struck by lightning while playing golf, and so on and so forth. There was a kind of fatalistic non-chalance in the way he explained that people get hurt mountain climbing.

I liked Al Read and found what I was beginning to think of as the "mountain climber personality type" very appealing.

Brooke, who had been listening to my conversation with Read, said, when he had moved off to help a client adjust a helmet, "Well, Dad, now we know one thing."

"What's that?"

"This thing is no slam dunk."

▲ ▲ ▲

The first day was called the basic school and it started out with the most elementary, basic stuff possible. There were six students and Read, our instructor. We rode a boat across Jenny Lake, then hiked up into the rocks where Read sat us in a circle and told us, in his calm, uninflected voice, that we wanted to be sure to drink a lot of water and wear sunblock. Then he picked up a rope and showed us how to coil it properly and how it should be carried. He told us how to care for a rope and inspect it. Then he showed us a climbing harness and demonstrated the proper way to wear it.

"You want to be sure," he said, "that you have buckled it properly." And then he showed us the correct way to buckle a harness. It was the sort of methodical, point-by-point style of instruction that has bored millions, and it all seemed terribly self-evident. But before any minds could wander too far, Read told us about the novice climber who had been killed, a couple of hundred yards from where we were sitting, when he fell out of an improperly buckled harness.

Talking about climbing, I learned, was like that. The conversation was never more than one easy transition from a calamity.

The sun climbed, the air turned warm, and we learned about

knots and how to tie into a harness with a figure eight, which is an elegant knot. Then we learned how to belay another climber.

It wasn't complicated. In fact, the way it was taught at Exum, it was simplicity itself. There are commonly used tools—hardware—that aid one climber who is belaying another. Tubes, they are called. Or Sticht plates. But at Exum they taught you how to do it using pure technique and your own body. A hip belay, it is called.

If your partner is roped to you, and you have taken a strong position and are executing a hip belay properly, with the rope around your waist and your belay hand—the one opposite the climber—is on the rope, then if he falls, you will catch him. He will fall, Read explained, only as far as the slack in the rope allows, if you are belaying from above, and as far as he is from his last piece of protection, and that far again, if he is the leader and you are belaying from below. I didn't understand that part but assumed it would become clear later, and it did.

But I understood the belay and how it worked, and I appreciated it for its simplicity. Do it right and your partner survives a fall and keeps on climbing. But if you don't do it right—if you take your belay hand off the rope because your mind wanders and your partner happens to fall at that moment—the results can be awful. If you don't take a good position and make sure you are securely anchored to the mountain, both you and your partner can be pulled off the mountain if he falls. There is a way to bring in rope, or let it out, so that your anchor hand is never off the rope, and we learned that. When it occurred to me that the climber I would most likely be holding on belay was my daughter, I asked Read to check my technique and correct it.

In the last hour before lunch, Read showed us the kind of "moves" a climber makes on rock. On a large boulder, he demonstrated the *lie back*, *smearing*, and *jamming*. Then we tried the moves and I got the first hint of something that would become increasingly obvious—Brooke would learn this faster than I did and she would get better at it than I ever would. Not only was I no longer her teacher; I wasn't able to keep up with her as a student.

I would have expected to be demoralized by this realization but for some reason I was not. She could lead and take risks as long as I was there to belay. There might not be much I could still teach her, I thought, but I could do that.

Making Moves

*Only one man was moving at a time; when he was firmly
planted the next advanced and so on. They had not however attached the additional rope to rocks.*

—Edward Whymper

B rooke and I sat next to each other on a wide, warm slab of
rock and shared our lunch with a marmot. It was late summer and he was obscenely fat from a diet of peanut butter,
cheese, gorp, and other treats he'd cadged from people at the
climbing school.

"So what do you think?" I said.

"I think it's cool, but do you think we'll be able to do that?" she
said, then pointed to a wall of vertical rock where a climber was
making what looked to me like very tentative moves up the face.
He was belayed from above, by another climber who was sitting
on a ledge with his feet braced against a rock. A third climber was
standing on the ledge, next to the belayer, tied into the rock. His
posture was so relaxed, and he hung out over the ledge with such
confidence, that you just knew he was the guide and instructor.

"That's Chuck Pratt," Read said.

"No kidding," I said.

"Who's he?" Brooke said.

"One of the best rock climbers in America," I said. "Maybe
the world."

I'm not sure how I knew that. Maybe from talking to Galen Rowell, a few years earlier, when I was following him around researching that story. Or perhaps from random reading, which I'd done in the years since I first saw the Grand and began nursing my climbing obsession.

"He was one of the early Yosemite pioneers," Read said to Brooke. "There was a group of those guys—Royal Robbins, Warren Harding, Tom Frost, and later on, Yvon Chouinard—who did some breakthrough climbing in the fifties and early sixties on the big walls like Half Dome and El Capitan."

Brooke looked over at the rock wall and studied the man standing on a narrow ledge, fifty feet up, as though it were a street corner and he was waiting on a bus. Only now, he was coiling the rope with brisk, efficient moves.

"So he's a star?" Brooke said.

Read smiled. "Well, it is hard to think of Chuck that way. He's a great climber and everyone who is interested in climbing has heard of him. He was sort of the prototypical Yosemite climber of the fifties and sixties. A physics major at Berkeley who dropped out and became a climbing bum. But a *great* climbing bum, one of the very best. They still talk about some of the climbs he made 30 years ago. Like the 'Crack of Doom.' But if you aren't interested in climbing, then his name doesn't mean anything to you."

"Nobody knows the names of any mountain climbers, do they?" Brooke said.

"Well," I said. "There's one."

"Ed Hillary," Read said.

I'd usually heard the great man called Sir Edmund Hillary, and occasionally Edmund Hillary. But never Ed. You don't hear people talking about Liz when they are referring to the Queen of England.

Read caught my look and smiled.

"He's a friend. I got to know him in Nepal, when I was working there."

"No kidding," I said and then, inevitably, "what's he like?" I could still recall, with considerable clarity, the way I felt when I read the account in *National Geographic*, at my grandparents' house, of how Hillary and Tenzing made their first ascent of Everest. It gave me a deep, urgent thrill then and I can still feel faint tremors of that same emotion today. The humble beekeeper from New Zealand had been my boyhood notion of a hero, even though I'd never seen a mountain.

"He's just what you've heard he is," Read said. "Modest, gracious, generous. He's a real gentleman. You know, in New Zealand, he is their national hero. You see his picture all over the place. Even on the money."

"Hard to imagine that happening here," I said. "I don't think we're likely to see Chuck Pratt's picture on a five-dollar bill."

Read laughed. "No," he said. "I don't think so. Chuck is the kind of guy who would rather have the money and let you keep the picture."

We finished our lunch and provided the marmot with a last handout or two. As we were walking to a rock face that rose 30 feet or so at a shallow angle, which is where we would begin our afternoon lessons, I said to Brooke, "You know, I had no idea. We're in the big time."

"What do you mean?"

"Well," I said, "Chuck Pratt is one of the guides here. And people call Sir Edmund Hillary 'Ed.' That's fairly impressive."

Brooke gave me the kind of tolerant smile she had seen on my face countless times when she'd been carrying on to me about some movie or rock star. The smile of someone who was too wise ever to be starstruck.

"Well don't let it dazzle you, Dad," she said. "I mean, you'll be belaying me this afternoon, and I want you to keep your mind on your work."

"Oh, I will," I said.

"And who knows? If you get good at this stuff, then maybe someday you can call him Ed, too."

▲ ▲ ▲

In the afternoon, we began using the things we had learned that morning, putting them together and actually climbing. We each tied in to our harness with a figure eight knot like we'd been taught. There were two of us on each rope. Once Read had checked every knot and the buckle of every harness, he climbed up the rock, trailing three ropes. He was not belayed but, then, this was such gently angled rock that he would have had to make an effort to fall.

We watched as he went up until he went over a small crest and was out of sight. After a minute or two, one of the ropes began to move. When all the slack was gone and the rope was tight to one climber's harness, he shouted up the rock, "That's me."

"On belay," we heard Read shout back down.

The climber—a young Marine on leave from Camp Pendleton—reached for a large crack in the rock, which was the first hold, and shouted, "Climbing."

"Climb on," Read shouted down to him.

The Marine started up the rock, moving aggressively. We watched him from below as he made his way up, working a lot harder than Al Read had, which was not surprising. But he was determined and in ten or fifteen minutes, he was up the rock.

A few moments after he disappeared over the crest, the rope began moving again, until it was tight to another climber who shouted, "That's me."

Brooke and I were on the third rope, and she was tied in ahead of me. Her voice sounded confident when she shouted, "That's me," and then, "Climbing." I was, no doubt, more nervous than she.

She moved up the rock using the holds Read had pointed out and the techniques he had demonstrated. She was careful, even tentative, and before she would put all of her weight on one foot, she would test the place where she had placed it, almost as though she suspected the rock might be rotten and would give way. But she kept moving and looking ahead for the next hold, and I watched the way fathers watch their children perform—proud and hoping that she wouldn't blow it. She didn't, and I felt an extra measure of relief when she moved over the crest and, a moment or two later, the slack began to disappear from my rope. She'd made it.

I followed the same route that she—and the others—had taken, trying to use the moves I'd learned that morning. It looked easy.

And it might have been if not for the height.

This is one of the fundamentals of climbing, especially when you are learning. Everything that is easy at ground level is hard at altitude. Everything that is hard at ground level is harder at altitude. The only thing that is easier at altitude than at ground level is . . . falling.

Place a four by four on the ground and try to walk from end to end.

Easy.

Now put the same beam between two sawhorses, four feet off the ground, and walk from end to end.

Harder. You move a little more tentatively, using your arms for balance.

Run the beam from the top of one building to the top of another, fifteen stories up.

Terrifying. Most people wouldn't even try it unless their lives depended on it.

So, even though the rock face was not steep and the moves were simple, my first attempt at rock climbing was no cinch. My mouth was dry, my heart was hammering, and my ears were ringing. I put my hands very carefully on the holds, making sure that I had as much of them as I could get my fingers around and that my grip was as firm as I could make it. I placed my feet carefully and tried to plaster as much of the sticky rubber sole as possible to the rock. Chuck Pratt himself had never been more deliberate, high on Half Dome with nowhere to go but up.

Though all the usual alarms were going off inside me, the same ones that warn you to step back from the guardrail at one of those scenic views on the highway, where the ground falls off into several hundred feet of air, I moved fairly quickly and with real purpose. But, then, I had an incentive. My daughter was watching.

"Nice job, Dad," she said when I made it to the top.

"Piece of cake," I lied and sat on a rock to catch my breath and wait for the alarms to stop ringing.

▲ ▲ ▲

We worked on increasingly steep rock as the afternoon went on. We did not go up anything that was sheer vertical, but the angle of the rock was enough to make a novice want to cling tightly, to hug the rock to keep from falling. This is precisely the wrong thing to do. There is much about climbing that is counterintuitive. (When I said this to my wife once, she answered, "Just about all of it, I'd say.") Leaning out from the rock is one of those things. Everything in you resists doing this but if you do it, you put all your weight over your feet and drive them into the rock. Climbing resembles skiing this way. It takes you a long time to accept the idea of leaning down the fall line of the mountain and getting your weight over the tips of your skis. But once you do it, you have much better balance and control and no longer feel like you are constantly on the verge of falling.

The same principle applies in climbing, but it takes time for your body to accept this counterintuitive notion. But by the end of the afternoon, Brooke and I were beginning to get the feeling. Now and then I would make a move I didn't think I could make, and Al, who would be on belay above me, would say mildly, "Nice work."

On what felt like one fairly steep section of rock, while I was studying my next move, Al said, "Okay, now I want you to let go of the rock."

"With my hands?" I said. I don't know what else he could have meant. Possibly my tail? The idea seemed preposterous.

"Yes," he said. "Just let go and pretend you are falling. I want you to learn to trust the belay."

Oh, I thought, and considered telling him that I trusted in the belay as surely as I trusted in the laws of gravity and diminishing returns. That my faith was whole, strong, and eternal. That no demonstration was necessary. I was forty feet off the ground and there was nothing beneath me but hard gray rock.

"Just let go," he said reassuringly. "I've got you."

My daughter was watching so I had no choice. I had to let go. Better to fall to my doom in front of her eyes than for her to see me wimp out.

It wasn't, of course, as tense and dramatic as that. I had a sure sense the belay would work and that Al Read had no reason to want me dead or crippled and every incentive, in fact, to avoid it. Still . . . I let go of the rock with reluctance.

I slipped down the face a couple of feet and then the rope came tight and I was hanging there, feeling the webbing of my harness cutting, slightly, into the flesh of my thighs and waist. No pain. I could have hung there like that for hours, I suppose, if I'd thought Read could hold the belay that long. I imagined him straining above me, then I heard his voice, calm as always.

"See," he said, anticipating my concern, "I can hold you without any trouble."

"I see."

"In climbing, you need to trust the belay."

"I do," I said, and thought, *Indeed I do.*

▲ ▲ ▲

Brooke went through the same drill and seemed to do it with fewer reservations and more confidence. The off-duty Marine was even bolder. Whatever he did, he was aggressive and he often tried to get up the rock face by main force.

"Use your legs," Read would tell him.

Brooke did not have to be told. Read's response, earlier in the day when we were signing the releases and I'd asked him if he thought Brooke would be all right, was "Why not?"

"Well," I'd said, haltingly, "she's young." I did not add, *and not very athletic.*

"Fifteen?" he said. "That's just the right age. Young enough that she doesn't think she knows it all and old enough to take coaching."

"And being a girl . . . I mean, upper body strength and all that?"

Read smiled tolerantly. "Some of the best rock climbers in the world are women. And women are almost always easier to teach. Better balance. Better attitude. They aren't trying to assault the rock and bring it to its knees. They are trying to dance right up the face, which is the way to go. Doesn't matter how big your arms and chest are, there is no way you can pull yourself up a mountain; you have to use your legs. Balance and coordination are more important than brute strength. It's the difference between pulling yourself forty feet up a rope and climbing the same distance on a ladder. Which would you rather do?"

"Ladder," I said. "For sure."

Read nodded, like a lawyer who'd just demolished a witness, and said, "She'll do fine."

And she did. I watched as she moved up a section of rock. She made each move carefully. She seemed unaware or unconcerned that she was being watched. And she did not try to wrestle the rock and pin it to the mat. She wasn't greedy and she took what the rock gave her. Even realizing that I wasn't the best judge of these things, I thought she was doing a good job.

Read agreed when I asked him during a break. "She's doing just fine. It's like I told you about girls and young women. They are a lot easier to teach. You don't have to get past all the macho stuff."

I considered the irony. I had, at first, been against her coming with me to climb the Grand because I thought she would hold me back. Now, clearly, she had started out ahead of me and I would probably never catch up. As much as I wanted her to succeed and to experience victories—she needed some, at this point in her life, outside the classroom—I wasn't sure I was ready for that.

▲ ▲ ▲

By late afternoon, we had done a couple short sections of rock which were steep enough that at the beginning of the day, I would have said we'd never climb them. Not with one day of training, anyway. We had learned to trust the belay. And we had done a couple of short rappels. And I was enjoying myself enormously. After a point in life, you don't get to try many entirely new things and when you find something new to try, you are usually frustrated by how hard it is to learn.

But I felt confident with my new skills and I liked the challenge of using them to get up a difficult-looking section of rock. Difficult for me, anyway, and this was one of the appealing things about the sport. You could always find a level where you were working at the limit of your skills, and then try to move it a little.

Brooke and I had been able to learn what Al Read taught and do what he asked us to do. We could, in short, climb. We weren't ready for the big walls of Yosemite, but we hadn't frozen up and quit at the basic school, either. This was something we could do and—best of all, to my thinking—something we could do together. I had begun, of late, to feel the first stirring of self-pity about losing my "little girls," especially Brooke, who was already away at school and into mid-adolescence, an age when your parents are increasingly an encumbrance and an embarrassment. Brooke and Hadley had less and less reason to spend time with me—I wasn't brushing their hair and reading them bedtime stories any longer. I wasn't coaching softball and teaching Sunday school. It had all gone by too fast. (This is one of the standard parents' laments; the other is, it can't go fast enough.) They both seemed more eager, these days, to get away from their parents than to spend time with them. I was grateful for anything that gave us this kind of day together.

So I was feeling good about things when we quit for the day and took the park service boat back across Jenny Lake to the Exum hut. Brooke was feeling good, too. We both were enjoying that pleasant glow that you get when you have accomplished something you thought difficult and that other people might not even be willing to try. We were pretty cocky, in other words.

The Climbing Culture

Gradient is the elixir of youth.   —Jerome Wyckoff

The clear blue skies of early morning had become obscured at mid-afternoon by the first thick, dirty clouds of an approaching mountain storm. By the time we quit for the day, a cold wind was blowing and you could feel the rain coming, just a few minutes away. It started on the boat ride across Jenny Lake, a few thin drops driven by the wind. By the time we were on the opposite shore, it was pouring.

Brooke and I put on our parkas and looked for Marsha and Hadley. There was no sign of their van, so we waited under the eaves of a park building, watching a line of headlights on the highway, coming south from Yellowstone Park.

"I imagine they got trapped in that," I said. "We might have a long wait."

Brooke shrugged. There was no hurry, except that it was cold.

After a couple of minutes, we were joined, in our dry spot under the eaves, by a man who looked to be in his late twenties. He had blond hair that almost reached his shoulders and that had been inexpertly cut—by a friend, maybe, or he might have done it himself. He hadn't shaved in several days but that would have been because he was conserving razor blades or hadn't gotten around to it, not because he was growing a beard. His face was lean, nearly gaunt, but he had the deep, intense climber's eyes. He was carrying a battered nylon pack with the top flap folded over a coiled climbing rope, and his parka was patched in several places with duct tape.

He gave us a quick look, inspecting our new packs and shiny parkas, and summed us right up.

"Climbing school?" he said. There was nothing hostile or condescending in his tone. It was, in fact, friendly. Almost eager.

"Yeah," I said. "First day."

He smiled and said, "Cool. How'd you like it?" He looked at Brooke when he said this.

"It was great," she said.

"Yeah," he said. "Nothing else like it. Live to climb."

Brooke and I both nodded and smiled. We weren't quite there yet, but we could dig it.

"Who was your instructor?"

"Al Read," Brooke said.

"No kidding. I didn't know he was taking people out anymore. He's head hog here, you know. One of the Exum owners, so he mostly stays in the office—administrating and like that. But he's been guiding here a long time."

"Since 1959," I said. "That's what he told me."

"I knew it was a long time," the man said. "He's one of the best."

"He's a good teacher," I said. "He gives you confidence."

"Yeah, that's it. He has that quiet thing going. Did he tell you about Nepal?"

"He said he lived there."

"And that he knew Hillary," Brooke added.

"Knew all of them. Hillary, Messner, Bonnington. Al was

there when Himalayan climbing was just beginning to open up, when the first American team made it up Everest, you know, and Unsold and Hornbein did that northern route and spent the night in the open at 28,000."

The man had so much enthusiasm that he could not stand still. He moved when he talked, bending his knees and waving his hands, nodding and shaking his head over the sheer magnificence and improbability of what he was describing.

"Can you believe that, man? Spending the night in the open at 28,000. I mean, *nobody* had ever done that before. Nobody believed it could be done. But they did it. And on the descent, too. Unsold lost all his toes, but they did it. Just unbelievable."

I remembered coming across an account of that climb, somewhere in my reading, and a story about how Unsold had found a boot maker in New Hampshire who built him a special pair of boots so he could keep climbing after he lost his toes. One of the legends of American climbing, Unsold had spent a lot of time in the Tetons and there was a section of one route up the Grand that was known as Unsold's Lieback.

Unsold was not much more than a name to me. Our companion under the eaves spoke his name the way Deadheads say Jerry. He was steeped in the religion of climbing and to him, the great ones—like Unsold and Messner—were deities.

"You know, Al Read might have done some great things if he hadn't had that close call on Dhaulagiri."

"Oh?" I said.

"You didn't hear about that?"

"No."

"Oh, man," he said. "Al is lucky he's still with us. Very, very lucky. I mean, two ways lucky, at least."

"What happened?" Brooke said.

"He was on this climb and he was really pushing. Went from 7,000 to something like 16,000 feet in one day and got both a cerebral and a pulmonary edema. Went into a coma. He was dying, man. They had to get him down, out of that altitude, and fast. So they evacuated him and there was a doctor at base camp who was able to do what needed to be done to keep him alive. For 36 hours, he was unconscious, and about as close to dying as you can get and still not be there. But he made it. And you know what?"

"What?" Brooke said. The way this man told the tale, you had to hear what came next.

"He was lucky in more ways than one. Lucky he survived and, maybe, lucky that he went into a coma and had to be evacuated. A week after they brought him down, seven people on his expedition were killed in an avalanche."

"God," Brooke said.

"Yeah. Al couldn't do the really high stuff anymore, but in a couple of ways, he's lucky he can still climb anything. You going out with him tomorrow?"

"I don't know," I said. "I wouldn't mind."

"He is good," the man said. "But you'll be with somebody good, no matter who you get."

"Are you with Exum?" I said.

"Me? Nah. I'm a good climber but I'm not a guide. That's something different, man. I just come here to climb, me and my buddy. That's our van over there." He pointed to a Volkswagen van that looked old enough to have survived Woodstock. It sagged on its springs, like a broken-down horse, and the pea-green sheet metal was patched in two or three dozen places with unpainted Bondo so the van looked like it had sores or, perhaps, the metallurgic equivalent of liver spots from age.

"Car trouble?" I said.

"Nah," he said, "I'm just waiting for my buddy. We came here this morning and he met some girl. They took off somewhere. He said he'd be back. I'd rather wait here than in the van. Smells nicer, you know."

Brooke seemed to enjoy this. The charms of the nomadic life were still pretty much theoretical to her. She'd been to a few concerts but as far as her father knew, she'd come home, or gone back to the dorm, when the concert was over.

"Where are you from?" I asked the man and it was obviously a tough question.

"California, I guess," he said after a while. "The Bay Area, you know. But we've been on the road for a while now."

Brooke asked him where he'd been and that, too, was a hard one.

"Well," he said, "right before this, we were in Yosemite for a while. That was awesome, but everybody knows that. And before, let's see, it was South Dakota. Outside of Rapid City, you know. Place is called the Needles, and the climbing is unbelievable. Big straight rocks that look like . . . well, you know, *needles*. Some really awesome 5.9 and 5.10 climbs where, when you get to the top, there is only room enough for one of you to stand. Fantastic.

"And, let's see, before that we were down in the desert. Joshua Tree. That is just some of the most incredible climbing. Great rock that comes right straight up out of the desert. Very rough, like climbing on sandpaper, so it's hard on the skin if you fall. But very, very cool climbing, if the desert can be cool; you know what I mean."

He rambled on, talking about other places where he and his buddy had climbed. The Sierras. Someplace outside of Las Vegas that, he said, was "way weird." Boulder, where "everyone with a rack and a pair of climbing shoes is out on the rock." And, of course, this place, the Tetons, which for rock jocks was one of the stations of the cross. Brooke was enchanted.

What was thrillingly possible for her was the stuff of nostalgia and missed opportunities for me. I could still remember feeling the spirit of Kerouac and sampling the romance of that life. But it was mostly long, pointless car trips fueled by amphetamines, alcohol, and endless talk. It was sufficient, back then, merely to be in motion. On the road.

Now people like our new friend led lives as nomadic as those of Kerouac and his idol, Cassady. But they also climbed, which was as simultaneously pointless and meaningful as driving all night down some long stretch of empty highway, on the way to nowhere. There was no point to the kind of climbing this young man did; the climbing *was* the point. I wondered what he did for money, which made me feel old.

"You work in town?" I said.

"Not yet," he said, and smiled broadly. "But I don't know how much longer I can hold out."

What did he do, Brooke asked, when he went to work.

"Wash dishes," he said.

Brooke frowned.

"It's the best job, for me," he said.

"Better than waiting tables?"

"Oh, yeah. I don't have to get all cleaned up and dressed and nobody screws with me."

"What about tips?"

"All the waiters and waitresses and bartenders feel sorry for me and share tips. And I get paid better, by the hour, than any of them. And, it is such a crummy job, I never mind quitting."

Clearly he'd thought this one through.

"Do you live in the van?"

"Sometimes. Right now, we're down the valley at the American Alpine Club hostel. It's cheap and clean. Nothing but climbers, so everybody is cool."

The rain was falling harder now and the wind was rising. It was cold under the eaves but none of us mentioned it. You don't worry about discomfort when you are living the life of an American nomad; that is for straight, suburban people.

The man talked on about the rootless life of a rock jock. He aimed his words at Brooke, not so much because he was trying to pick her up (I think) but because she was young and would, therefore, understand. I was on the verge of qualifying for membership in the AARP (an organization I despised even more than I hated being old enough to join it), so I was immediately DQed from a conversation about living in Volkswagen buses and washing dishes for a living. I listened and recalled the crack somebody once made about how, at either extreme of the economic spectrum, there exists a leisure class, and I wondered if Brooke was ever tempted to quit school and join the one at the low end of the pole. I found myself worrying, absurdly, about yet another danger in bringing her along on this little stunt of mine. Maybe instead of falling off the mountain, she would fall in love with mountains, drop out, and become a rock-climbing gypsy, turning her back on her prep school education and all her parents' plans.

I was, of course, projecting. At least that is what I think they call it: imagining what I would have done in her place. I was also acting like a damned fool, something that fathers who dote on their daughters routinely do when their girls reach a certain age. Mine were going to leave me soon, both of them, for something and it didn't necessarily have to be a boy. In my foolish, but sincere, condition I now saw climbing—the kind we had been doing all day—not as something we could share but as a rival, one I could never beat.

It was probably just the rain, my weariness, the strangeness of both the place and our companion. Still, I looked out toward the highway, hoping to see Marsha and Hadley pulling off the highway onto the access road.

▲ ▲ ▲

I had stopped paying attention to our talkative companion, and when I tuned him back in, I discovered he was telling Brooke stories from the days when Chuck Pratt—plainly a hero of his—and other climbers were doing great deeds in Yosemite. In his passion for climbing, and everything about it, he reminded me of those boys who love baseball and in their devotion, memorize statistics from seasons that even the sportswriters have forgotten. They could tell you how many homers Mickey Mantle hit the same season Maris hit 61, just like our new friend could remember, and describe, the first ascents in Yosemite, made by Chuck Pratt, Warren Harding, Royal Robbins, Tom Frost, and his other heroes.

It was actually pleasant to listen to him tell those stories. He had both enthusiasm and humor, and he wanted other people to feel the way he did about the lore. I was paying more attention to the highway than his words when I realized he was telling a story about someone who had fallen in Yosemite and been killed.

"It was a kid," the man was saying, "doing a rappel in the backcountry. Some of the experienced climbers—Warren Harding and them—volunteered to go in and recover the body, you know, but the rangers said, 'no way.' "

"How come?" Brooke interrupted.

"Too dangerous. They figured one body back in there was bad enough. Any more and it would be bad PR for the park. So the body stayed in there. All winter long."

"Jeez."

"Yeah. And it was still in there, what was left of it, the next spring, when Yvon Chouinard and Steve Roper went in there to do a one-day climb of this route called Arrow Chimney. They knew they were going to have to climb right past what was left of the dude, and that kind of spooked them. But they went anyway and Roper was leading when they got to the place where the remains were.

"They're climbing—it's a steep pitch—and Yvon can't see what's going on but he knows that Roper is in the right place up above him. He's waiting to hear something and finally, he can't stand it anymore so he hollers up, 'You okay?'

"And Roper hollers back down, 'Yeah, I'm okay.'

"But Chouinard isn't satisfied, you see. He *has* to know. So he hollers back up, 'What's it like?'

"And for a minute or two, Roper doesn't say anything. Chouinard is thinking that maybe he's just too freaked out to even talk. Then, finally, Roper hollers back down, 'Damn.'

"And Chouinard hollers, '*What?* What is it?' He's kind of freaked now himself.

" 'His parka is too goddamned small.' "

▲ ▲ ▲

We left the man a few minutes later, still standing under the eaves, smiling and still full of stories to tell, when Marsha and Hadley pulled up.

"Good luck," he said, "I hope you get someone interesting, like Chuck Pratt, tomorrow."

We said we'd see him again, but we never did.

We had a good evening, the four of us, eating dinner and telling each other our stories from the day. Hadley and Marsha had seen the sights and the animals of Yellowstone, including a large herd of buffalo. Hadley, who had always been an animal person, said it was the best day of her life.

We were all tired so we went to bed early. Before I went to sleep, my wife and I talked a little. She wanted to know if there was anything I had to tell her.

"You mean something I couldn't say in front of Brooke?"

"Yes," she said.

"Nope. We told you every bit of it. In more detail than most people would be willing to put up with."

Which was true. Both Brooke and I had been especially voluble. We were charged up and we described every move and just about every minute of the day, including meeting our friend under the eaves. But we'd both left out his story about the parka that didn't fit. And I didn't tell it now, either.

Man-made Obstacles

What have these lonely mountains worth revealing?
—Emily Brontë

In the morning, we went back to the area called Guides' Rocks with an instructor who was not Chuck Pratt. Our new teacher was tough and even a little abrasive, telling us exactly where to sit and then standing in front of us with his hands on his hips and, instead of talking to us conversationally the way Al Read had done, lecturing us like a hard-nosed football coach. He was forceful and you suspected that if he were not dealing with paying clients, he would have adopted entirely the manners of a drill sergeant.

Which would have been fine with me—this was serious business—except that he seemed to have a problem with Brooke, asking her questions and then finding something to mock or criticize in her answers. For the first hour or so, I thought it was because she was the only kid in the group, so I mentally cut him a little slack. I imagined that he'd probably had some unpleasant experiences with bored kids, brought here by their parents and dropped off for a few days. I figured he would come around.

The Marine was still part of our group. The other three people who had been with us did not return. They had, evidently, signed up for just one day or they had seen enough. We were joined by two young men—three or four years older than Brooke, I guessed—who were from Los Angeles, where they spent a lot of time in climbing gyms. I knew this because they made sure everyone knew it.

Indoor climbing walls were still a relatively new thing back then. Genuine mountain guides, like those at Exum, were (and to a degree, still are) agnostic on the subject of indoor walls. You can learn how to make some very athletic moves on them, this much is undeniable. But it is a sterile, laboratory environment that teaches you no outdoor skills. Also, people who come out of the gyms tend not to feel the proper respect for real mountains.

These two young men were both skillful and arrogant. They did not bother to conceal a feeling that they were better climbers than our instructor and wasting their time in his class, which they were taking simply because that was the only way they could go, with Exum, to the summit of the Grand. They barely paid attention during the review, and when the instructor showed us the route we would be taking up a fairly nasty-looking (to me) piece of vertical rock, they glanced at it as though it was hardly worth the look.

Our instructor sized these two up, which wasn't hard, and I assumed that also accounted for his mood. He didn't like kids, I thought, and he didn't like hotshots. The Marine and I were probably all right.

"What's his problem?" Brooke whispered to me, during the break, before we started climbing.

"I don't know," I said. "Maybe he's just having a bad day."

"Yeah," she said. "Maybe."

After the break, the instructor roped up and with the Marine on belay, began climbing up the rock, along a deep crack, and demonstrating a technique called jamming, where you slip your extended hand into a crack, then make a fist that becomes your hold. You free your hand by extending your fingers again. The instructor began putting in various pieces of protection as he went up—mostly spring-operated camming devices called friends, that went into the crack when the spring was loaded and then became a wedge when the spring was let off. He would attach a carabiner to the friend, run the rope through the carabiner, and explain that if he now fell, it would be only as far as he was above that piece of protection and then that far again. If he was ten feet above this friend, then, and he fell, he would drop ten feet and then another ten before the rope went taut and the Marine caught him on the belay. He explained it carefully and clearly. He was a good teacher; I gave him that.

And a good climber, though the boys from the L.A. gym made it clear that they were not impressed. Their attention and their eyes wandered. Brooke and I watched the instructor all the way to a ledge, about 60 feet up, where he tied himself in. The Marine's eyes never left the instructor until he called down, "Off belay."

"Belay off," the Marine answered. He released the rope.

One of the L.A. gym climbers was next.

"Go for it," his partner said.

"No fear," the young man said. He gave his partner a high five and then he attacked the rock.

He moved quickly, showing off, and when he reached the first piece of protection, he moved past it without unclipping from the carabiner. A few feet farther up the rock, the rope brought him up short.

"Forget something?" the instructor said. He'd warned us about this.

"Yeah. I guess so."

"You're not top roping in some gym," the instructor said.

"I know."

"Well, try not to forget."

I climbed before Brooke and had to remind myself to lean back from the rock and put my weight over my feet. I moved slowly and tentatively. About halfway up, I tried to hug the rock. My feet lost traction, slid from the rock, and were dangling uselessly beneath me. The fingers of one hand were wrapped like a vice around a flake of rock high above my head. The other hand was in a crack at about eye level.

I kicked, frantically, hoping my toes would find something to stand on and take up some of the strain. But my feet slipped off the rock like it was greased. The hand that was jammed in the crack didn't seem to be holding any load, so I pulled it out and reached for another, higher crack. I was holding all my weight up with the fingers of one hand, and I could feel those fingers coming loose and there wasn't anything I could do about it. I was falling.

I did not panic or experience any overwhelming sense of terror. One second I was still connected to the rock and then . . . I wasn't. I was falling, still scrambling with hands and feet, trying to find some purchase. But falling. Out of control. No longer plastered to the rock, moving up slowly, but going down fast.

But it was over after I'd gone a few feet. The belay caught and I was hanging there, looking at the rock, with one knee bloody, a cut lip, a chipped tooth, and a feeling of both embarrassment and relief. I wasn't happy to be the first person in our group to fall, but I was relieved to have taken my first real fall. It was something I wouldn't have to do again. I liked knowing, viscerally, that the belay worked. Up until now, it had been strictly theory. I took a couple of deep breaths and said I was fine when the instructor asked.

"Don't hug the rock," he said. "Lean out."

"Right."

When I got to the ledge, where the Marine and the two gym climbers were waiting, the instructor clipped me into the rock without a word.

Now it was Brooke's turn. Five pairs of adult male eyes looked down on her as she started up. She moved deliberately, putting her hands and feet where she'd seen the instructor put his.

She made it to the first piece of protection, carefully unclipped, took the friend from the crack, and hung it from a sling that was draped across her body. Since she was the last person climbing, she was clearing the protection as she went. And being careful to do it right. She leaned back and studied the rock face above, looking for the next good hold.

"Let's go," the instructor shouted down. "Keep moving. We'd like to finish this pitch before lunch, if you don't mind."

I could feel the heat rising inside me and taste something sour in my throat.

Brooke did not say anything and neither did I. But I badly wanted to. This guy was bullying her, like some playground creep. She was working harder and making fewer mistakes than any of us except, perhaps, the Marine. I felt myself on the edge of blurting something—I'd never minded confrontations, where my daughters were concerned—but we were 60 feet off the ground, crowded onto a little six-inch rock ledge. This was neither the time nor, certainly, the place. I swallowed the little wad of bile in the back of my throat.

I looked down at Brooke, and I could see that she was moving with an extra measure of determination. She was angry. I recognized the look because I'd gotten it myself, many times, after scolding her.

"Any time," the instructor said when she reached the next piece of protection, carefully unclipped, then freed the piece from the rock and clipped it to the sling. Now I got it. The sarcasm was so gratuitous, and so childish, that I suddenly understood. It wasn't because she was a kid; it was because she was a girl.

The way this guy saw it, Brooke wouldn't be able to do anything right. Even he could not teach her how to not be a girl.

I stood on my little section of the crowded ledge, seething, while she made the last few feet of her climb. On flat ground, I thought, I would break his face.

"Good job," the Marine said when Brooke reached the ledge. The instructor did not say anything to her, merely tied her into the rock, took her off belay, and started up the next pitch to the top.

The two L.A. gym rats followed him. Then the Marine. When Brooke and I were alone on the ledge, I said, "Listen . . ."

"I know, Dad," she said. "He's a jerk."

"And I'm going to tell him about it."

She shook her head, making her long blonde hair dance. "No, please."

"Well, we'll go back to the hut after this pitch and I'll complain to Al, tell him we want another instructor . . ."

"No," she said. "Please don't do that. I'll be fine. I can handle it."

"We can come back tomorrow, with somebody different."

"It's not that big a deal," she said. "Let's just climb and have fun." She'd never spoken to me this firmly and it made an impression. I realized that I had no idea how many battles like this one she'd fought. Also that among the many things that come to an end as your child grows older is your ability to protect her from the world's insults.

"All right," I said and noticed that I was trembling. And it was not from fear. "Then, I'll need to get my mind on what I'm doing."

"That's what I do," she said.

▲ ▲ ▲

The instructor did not say anything sarcastic to Brooke about her pace when she was coming up the second pitch, and she was just as deliberate as she had been on the first. She wasn't going to be rushed by this guy and I admired that. Most people—especially young people—would have been shamed into hurrying. When she made it to the top and went off belay, the instructor nodded at her. He couldn't bring himself to say anything, but you could take the nod as a compliment of sorts.

Brooke seemed to have put it behind her at lunch. We fed gorp to another fat marmot—or maybe it was the same one and he knew a mark when he found one—and talked to the Marine, who joined us and was astonished that Brooke was my daughter. Since she was only a couple of years younger than he, that meant I had to be *old*.

"God," he said, "I hope I'm still doing stuff like this when I'm your age."

It was one of those comments that you could take either of two ways, and I knew which way I wanted to take it.

▲ ▲ ▲

We began the afternoon on rock that was slightly steeper and slightly smoother than what we had climbed in the morning. The holds were small and you had to extend yourself and trust your balance—and the belay—20, 40, and then 60 feet off the ground. Even the gym rats were straining.

One of them got cute and tried to "dyno," across a slick section of rock. This is when you use the last hold to get some purchase and then fling yourself across the rock, hoping to grab another hold that is beyond your reach. The young man from L.A. couldn't quite get his fingers wrapped around the little three-inch nub of rock he was trying for. He fell.

The instructor was belaying and caught the man after he'd fallen four or five feet and skinned a knee.

"Nice try, hero," he said.

The man from L.A. did not answer. He looked at his bloody knee with dismay and got himself repositioned for another try.

"If you'll look to your left, please?" the instructor said.

The man looked to his left.

"Notice the nice crack that you can reach easily without leaving your feet."

The man found the crack and used it for a handhold to make his next move.

"Much better," the instructor said. "Save the gymnastics for the gym."

Brooke was standing next to me, watching the man from L.A. move up the rock, and I whispered to her, "Maybe our guide is an equal-opportunity jerk."

"No," she whispered back. "He's only yelled at me and the tag team from L.A. So I guess he likes Marines and old guys."

I struggled when it was my turn. Got too deep into an open-book sort of crack and had to work my way out by going down and starting over. The instructor either thought it was an honest mistake or so dumb it wasn't worth even a disdainful remark. By the time I made it to the end of the first pitch and tied in, the first clouds were beginning to gather and obscure the peaks above us.

A storm was coming, possibly one with lightning. Our group of six climbers was halfway up a serious, two-pitch rock climb. And, actually, one of our group, Brooke, had not climbed the first pitch yet. We needed to move.

We all knew this, including Brooke, with all of us watching both her and the sky. I wanted to shout something to her, a few sappy words of fatherly encouragement, but I had enough sense not to. She was on her own.

I bit my swollen lip and tried to will a good performance out of her, the way I had from the third-base coaching box during a lot of close softball games. The stakes here, of course, were a lot higher . . . or maybe not.

I silently urged her to move quickly . . . but not too quickly.

Be decisive, I thought. But not too decisive.

I also worked on willing the instructor to keep his mouth shut.

Brooke moved nicely up to the first piece of protection, un-clipped, worked the friend out of the crack, and clipped it to her sling.

"Nice," the Marine said softly. He was on her side. Probably he didn't get to share a bag of gorp with many blondes at Camp Pendleton.

"Keep moving," the instructor said but without malice, merely urging her along, like a good coach should.

She made it to the next piece of protection, still moving well, and then into the open book. I reminded her, silently, not to follow her father's example.

She made it without getting herself in, literally, too deep, and then came on fast, cleaning the protection as she went. There was a bulge, not quite an overhang, just below the ledge, and when she reached that, the instructor said, "Don't hug it now, lean back and use your legs." He was encouraging her now like a supportive coach.

She made the last move, stood on the ledge, clipped in, and said, "Off belay."

I felt like I could breathe again.

"Nice job," the instructor said. Then to the rest of us, "Okay, I don't like being stuck out here on the side of this mountain in the rain and lightning. So let's move as fast as we can, without getting careless." At this point he looked sternly at the gym rats from L.A. "Then when we get to the top, we'll rappel back down to our packs and put on our rain gear."

The rain had just begun when we finished the rappel. Brooke, the Marine, and I all put on rain gear. The gym rats hadn't brought any. The instructor shook his head and said, "You never—and I mean, never—go into the mountains without proper clothing and equipment. It might be August but it can still get cold enough in the mountains for you to die from hypothermia. Do you know what that is?"

They nodded, sullenly, in unison.

"Your core body temperature drops," the instructor went on, as though he hadn't noticed or didn't believe the gesture, "and you can't stop it because you are uninsulated and the wind is stripping heat away from you. And you die. Happens all the time and it shouldn't *ever* happen. I can understand a fall. That's part of climbing and when it happens, too bad but you understood the risks. Or you should have, anyway. But dying from hypothermia because you didn't pack any foul-weather gear . . . man, that is just dumb."

He was on the verge of sending the two climbers, who had lost their swagger, down to the dock where they could catch the boat back across Jenny Lake to the Exum hut. But the rain stopped, suddenly. The storm clouds broke up and the sun reappeared. Brooke, the Marine, and I took off our parkas and put them back in our packs. Then we all made the last, most difficult climb of the day. Brooke went first, after the instructor, this time, followed by the Marine. I was next. The two young men from L.A., now sulking, were last.

Brooke did fine and I made it without falling or getting myself squeezed too tight in an open book. We were happy and tired coming down. We probably should have felt a sense of self-confidence, but we didn't. Not entirely, anyway. We were more like students who had taken an exam and thought we'd done well but wouldn't be sure until the grades were posted. This is because we had been told, before we left the hut in the morning, that our instructor would be watching our performance and evaluating it to determine whether or not we were capable of attempting the Grand.

"Do you think he'll let us go?" Brooke said. We were starting down the trail. The instructor was ahead of us, out of hearing.

"Sure," I said. "Why not?"

"I don't know," she said.

"We did fine."

"I guess."

"And you stood up to him, in just the right way."

"That's what I'm worried about."

I began to get angry all over again and to feel about the instructor the way I had that morning. I imagined him saying we were not qualified—or, worse, that I was and Brooke wasn't—for some contrived reason. She was too slow, for instance.

"We'll be all right," I said.

The ride back across the lake had been upbeat and nearly festive the day before. Today, it was quiet. Nearly grim. The two gym rats were still sulking and neither the instructor nor Brooke seemed in a mood for small talk. She was worried about the evaluation. He seemed to have circled all the way back to his morning mood, and I wondered if he had trouble at home—a wife just waiting to give him hell.

The Marine and I talked a little but it was generally a quiet ride, and for the first time, I got a hint of how a day—or a long expedition—in the mountains could turn on personality differences.

We had to turn in helmets and ropes at the Exum hut. I spoke to the woman behind the desk and reminded her that Brooke and I still wanted to try for the Grand.

"Yes," she said. "I understand."

I mentioned the date, slightly over a week away.

"That's right," she said.

"Well . . ." I said, tentatively, "we just finished the intermediate school and I'm wondering if we qualified for the Grand."

"Oh, yes," she said. "I heard you both did fine."

"Great," I said, trying not to sound too relieved. I didn't want her to think I doubted myself. Or my daughter.

"Just be here early in the morning. Eight o'clock. And make sure you have everything on the check list."

"Right," I said. "Any idea of who our guide will be?"

"No," she said. "Not yet."

"Same man we had today?" I said, trying to make it sound like an innocent question.

"Probably not," she said. "He doesn't do many overnights."

Because, I maliciously thought, he has to get home to the woman who makes him so miserable.

"All right," I said. "We'll see you at eight o'clock."

"Just pray for good weather," she said.

"We will. For sure."

Brooke was waiting for me outside the hut and we walked together, down the trail to the access road where we would be meeting Marsha and Hadley. They had gone rafting while we were climbing.

"Well, I'm proud of you," I said. "You had to deal with more than just climbing and you did fine."

"He wasn't that bad," she said. "Anyway, the climbing was great."

"Yes," I said, "it sure was. Tough, too."

"I don't know why some guys have to act that way," she said. "You know what I mean."

"Yes."

"I mean, what *is* his problem?"

"I don't know," I said. "But I'll tell you something."

"What's that?"

"I might have been the same way, once upon a time. Worse, maybe."

"Oh, come on."

"I mean it."

She didn't say anything for a while. Finally she said, "Well, what changed?"

"What do you mean?"

"How come you aren't like that guy anymore? How come you can coach a girls softball team and like that?"

"That's easy," I said. "It's because I have daughters."

Waiting on the Grand

In that exquisite moment before the hard move, when one looks and understands, may lie an answer to the question why one climbs. —Gwen Moffat, 1961

We had a week between finishing the Exum school and our scheduled climb of the Grand. I had planned for this and made reservations for a week at a "guest ranch" (this is what they are calling dude ranches, these days) in Big Sky, Montana. The place was called Lone Mountain Ranch and I'd been to three or four conferences there when my column on the outdoors became a column about the environment. I had learned things—and more important, made contacts—at these conferences, but I'd also enjoyed myself (fishing mostly) and watched the ordinary guests enjoying themselves. There were a lot of families at Lone Mountain, and it made a sweet scene when one of them would come down to the corral in the morning, mount up, and head out into the hills following one of the wranglers. I had wanted to do this with my wife and girls since that first conference, and this was the year.

Big Sky was a five- or six-hour drive from Jackson, through the Teton Pass and then across miles and miles of flat Idaho potato farming country. I could look back and see the profile of the Grand outlined against the sky.

"It's not going anywhere, Dad," Hadley said. She was 12 and hip enough now to tease me when she found a weakness.

"Just checking," I said.

"You keep your eyes on the road," Marsha said, "we'll watch your mountain for you."

We swung north and crossed the Henry's Fork, a little downstream from the spot where I'd been fishing years earlier when I'd first laid eyes on the Grand and begun nourishing this obsession. This was easily my favorite trout stream so we detoured, slightly, so I could show everyone the famous Harriman Ranch, which was now included in a small state park. At one time, the Harrimans of Union Pacific fame and fortune had lived here, on the banks of one of the best trout pools on the river with a view, across miles of flat prairie, of the Tetons. It was, to my mind, one of the most magical parcels of real estate anywhere. But as my girls liked to remind me, not everyone cared about trout fishing and mountains the way I did.

From the Henry's Fork, we drove through a corner of Yellowstone Park. There was still evidence of the great fires that had burned through the park, a couple of years earlier.

"Oh, man," Brooke said when we came on a hillside of dead trees, their trunks blackened by fire. "How bad is that?"

There was something undeniably sobering about the acres and acres of scorched spars. But the effect was softened by the green of young plants and saplings growing in earth that the fires had exposed.

The highway followed the Gallatin River downstream, until we reached the turnoff for Big Sky. We arrived at Lone Mountain Ranch in time for cocktails and dinner.

We had a log cabin with a loft, which Brooke and Hadley thought was cool. They slept up there. Marsha and I had the big bedroom below. There was a woodstove and it was cold enough, on a clear night in late August, that I built a fire before bedtime. We were, I think, all excited to be where we were and glad to be there together. Family vacations are supposed to follow the hell-is-suburbia script of one of those Chevy Chase movies where the kids are bored and quarrelsome, the wife is long-suffering, and the husband is hopelessly obtuse. But we were having fun . . . so far. In the morning we would be going riding, and we were all looking forward to it, especially Hadley.

As it turned out, we were following our own script for disaster. An hour after we'd mounted up and taken a trail through a vast Montana meadow full of blooming lupine and Indian paintbrush, it became clear that the years and years of expensive injections Brooke had been getting for her allergies were not working. Not, at least, when the antigen came from a horse. Her face swelled, like a budding flower, and turned a bright, hot shade of red. Her eyes were squeezed into slits the width of nickels. We turned around and by the time we were back at the corral, she could barely breathe. She took a bath, medicated herself with Benadryl, and went to bed.

She felt terrible and the rest of us were miserable for her.

Most of what you do at a dude ranch involves horses and riding, and I wondered if Brooke had any good alternatives to sitting around playing solitaire while the rest of us were off enjoying ourselves. There were some hikes, one of the wranglers told me, but somehow, walking a trail that she could have been riding seemed like a bad solution. This was the west and you were meant to see it from horseback.

She could fish in the Gallatin, the wrangler suggested, if she liked to fish, that is.

She did; but not enough to spend a week fishing alone.

"And," the man said, "well, it's kind of a long shot . . ."

"What?" I asked.

"Well, there's a fellow who comes in. He doesn't work for the ranch, understand, but they let him come in and see if there's any guests who're interested."

"In what?"

"Rock climbing."

"You're kidding," I said.

"I know," the wrangler said, "it's crazy . . .

"It's perfect," I said, and the wrangler gave me a look. What kind of father thinks the perfect thing for an ailing daughter is a little rock climbing with a perfect stranger in a place far from home? Further proof that those eastern people are sick sumbitches.

▲ ▲ ▲

The week that we had planned to spend together turned out to be like most other weeks. We went in different directions all day, then got together at the dinner table.

But we split up in interesting ways. One day Brooke and I went climbing on a tall chimney a few miles down the Gallatin, while Hadley and Marsha went riding. On another day Brooke went climbing with the guide while I went riding with Marsha and Hadley and a wrangler, 10,000 feet up into the Madisons. And one day Brooke and I drove to the Henry's Fork and fished and gazed at the distant Tetons, slightly indistinct in the shimmering, late summer air.

Late in the week, Marsha and Hadley and I took another trail ride, up into the Spanish Peaks. I'd learned how to ride well enough to get along on hunting trips when it was necessary, but I wasn't much good and I wouldn't have considered a day of trail riding for pleasure on my own. But with Hadley it was different. She was still a kid and an enthusiast. The wrangler plainly enjoyed her company and let her ride ahead as though she were our scout. She had good eyes, he told her, after she had spotted a cow moose concealed with her calf in the shadows of a stand of lodgepole. And again, when she rode back down the trail and told the rest of us to come up slowly so we wouldn't spook the elk she'd found grazing in a small meadow.

Late in the day, she held up and waited for me to join her where the trail crossed a ridgeline. I assumed she'd spotted another animal up ahead, but when I reined in next to her, she pointed off toward the horizon where the Grand stood out with remarkable clarity.

"You can relax, Dad," she said. "It's still there."

"Thanks, kid," I said. "I can't tell you how relieved I am."

"Just four more days. Then you and Brooke will be standing on the top."

"That's right," I said. "You sure you don't want to go?"

"Not unless I can ride a horse," she said.

In an odd way, things were working out in spite of Brooke's illness. Or, perhaps, because of it. Brooke had mountains; Hadley had horses.

The wrangler joined us on the ridge and said to Hadley, "You spot something with them sharp eyes of yours?"

"Just that mountain."

"Yeah," the wrangler said, "she's a big one, ain't she?"

"My dad's going to climb it," Hadley said, in a way that made me feel both proud and a little foolish.

"No kidding?"

"I'm going to *try*," I said.

"When?"

"Four days. On my fiftieth birthday."

"Well, good on you," the wrangler said. "You'd never in hell catch me doing that. But I think it's fine."

"My sister's going, too," Hadley said.

"The one got sick from the horses?"

"That's her."

"How come you're not going? You could get up ahead and scout for the rest of them."

Hadley shook her head. "That's my sister's thing. I told my dad I'd go with them if I could ride my horse."

"You and me, both, scout," the wrangler said. "You'd have to put something real special on top of that thing before I'd try to climb up and get it."

▲ ▲ ▲

I usually enjoyed it when the subject of what Brooke and I were planning came up, and it drew that kind of reaction. It gave me a kind of cheap little thrill, a fleeting but very smug sense of superiority. After it passed, I would feel slightly ashamed and tell myself that if I was motivated strictly by exhibitionism, then I ought to bag it right now. This led me to an examination of my own motives, something I didn't do very well. But I came back, inevitably, to the same conclusion. When it first occurred to me to try climbing, and for the years afterward that I secretly cultivated the idea, I had no idea of doing it to show off. It might have been a dumb, childish idea, but it wasn't motivated by vanity.

Which leads, of course, to the next question: why, then *did* I want to do it?

Why climb mountains? The question has been asked over and over, and evidently, no one has ever supplied a very good answer because people are still asking. George Leigh Mallory gave the most famous answer when he blew off a persistent journalist, who insisted on knowing *why* Mallory wanted to climb Everest, with the wonderfully opaque and immortal line: "Because it is there."

If you don't get it, there is no explaining it.

I have thought for a long time that the best, most conclusive answer a climber could give a non-climber who asks that question would be: "Have you ever tried it?"

But this does not explain why a non-climber would feel compelled to try a (relatively) big mountain. Especially one who is well beyond the prime climbing years, entirely inexperienced, and carrying the usual burden of real-life responsibilities.

I had not thought much—maybe not at all—about this question as long as climbing was strictly speculative. But now that it was getting closer and assuming the hard contours of reality, I tried to come up with some kind of rationale for this thing I was about to do. I thought about it, after we left the ridgeline with its dramatic view of the Grand that remained a fading afterimage on my mind during the long ride back down the trail.

What is it about mountains?

Even a badly educated layman can find evidence to support an argument that mountains touch something spiritual in us.

I will lift up mine eyes unto the hills
From whence commeth my strength.

We'd memorized those lines from the book of Psalms, my kids and I, when I taught Sunday school.

And, of course, the Greeks made Mount Olympus the dwelling place of their gods. Even in the modern age, after the death of God, Thomas Mann found corruption in *Death in Venice*, but a kind of consumptive transcendence on *The Magic Mountain*.

For the Buddhists in Tibet, the mountains are not mere homes to the gods; they *are* gods.

The kind of sensibility that longs after spirituality without a divinity is drawn by the purity of mountains, with their clean, thin air and the hard distance between their peaks and the fleshy world of the valleys.

But while the spiritual pull of the mountains is undeniable, this doesn't explain why some people feel the urge to climb them. In fact, mountain climbing was pretty much unheard of in the Age of Faith and did not really get going until the Age of Reason. Of course, they had better equipment then.

Mallory, who stands for a whole generation of climbers, was a child of the Enlightenment, though his "because it is there" crack betrays the disillusionment and cynicism of the Great

War. Still, that generation of climbers had a superficially plausible rationale for what they were doing. They were going where no man (or woman) had ever been. They were explorers.

That won't wash for climbers of this era, especially not for those who take it up late in life and climb mountains where you practically have to make a reservation to get on. Like golfers who call ahead for a tee time, people who climb the Matterhorn these days reserve a summit time. But there are inevitable traffic jams and some parties climb through.

This is not, by any stretch, exploration.

So what is it?

The obvious—and embarrassing—answer is that it is a stunt. Showing off. But I had already concluded that it was more than that, even if I had discovered the guilty pleasures of exhibitionism . . . *and I hadn't even climbed the mountain yet.*

I brooded about this, as I brought up the end of our string of horses, riding back down a narrow trail to the valley, where we would clean up and join Brooke for a nice dinner in Lone Mountain's dining room.

Some of it, of course, was risk. Pure and simple. Risk and fear. *Risk is a part of climbing,* you hear that all the time and read it on the brochures that you get from, for example, Exum Mountain Guides. Of course it is. But the formulation makes it sound as though risk is an unfortunate by-product of climbing, something one learns to put up with. Sort of like saying, *Intoxication is a part of drinking whiskey.*

The undeniable truth is that risk lies at the heart of the appeal of mountain climbing. There may be other reasons to climb mountains, but they are fairly tepid by comparison. It is risk that makes climbing so ineffably seductive. Trying to imagine climbing without risk is like trying to imagine seduction without sex.

Taking risks and surviving is, quite simply, exhilarating. The sensation of danger is undeniably alluring and explains why amusement parks stay in business, selling tickets to the roller-coaster ride. You come away with a glow, happy to be alive. The greater, more genuine, and sustained the risk, the more profound the sensation. There are simulated risks, cheap thrills, like rides on the roller coaster, which you can buy for a couple of bucks and, then, there is genuine risk.

There is a vast and essential difference between climbing and, say, bungee jumping. When you jump with a "reputable" outfit (if that word applies) you will scare the bejesus out of yourself, but there is really no chance that you will be killed or injured. All the dangerous variables have been accounted for and are under the control of others. You are merely a paying passenger, along for the ride. Destination nowhere. The point of this trip is a simple adrenaline rush, pure sensation which you will have forgotten in an hour.

When you climb, on the other hand, you take genuine risks and you manage them. You are hoping to get right up next to the edge of your ability and to dance there, in control, but just barely. You not only feel the pump of danger but also a warm feeling of pride in having survived not merely by luck (which some people feel every time a passenger jet's wheels touch ground) or through grace, but from some combination of your own cool and skill. This, anyway, is the ideal. And it probably accounts for a lot of climbing's appeal. Somewhere in my random and undisciplined reading about climbing, I came across a line to the effect that climbing and bullfighting were the only true sports. Pretty thick and arch (which makes me think it might be Hemingway) but it holds a nugget.

Still, while all climbing is—in the locutions of the legal releases you sign—inherently risky, it is not suicidal or, probably, even as dangerous in an actuarial sense as some jobs. Coal mining or tree felling, for instance. And you don't see young college-educated people seeking out thrilling experiences in the West Virginia mines or the Oregon logging woods. There are no apparel companies turning out stuff with the coal miner or lumberjack look.

Which is to say, there is more to climbing than the possibility of a fall, frostbite, avalanche, and the other risks you take in the mountains.

I thought about this all the way down to the trailhead where we dismounted, unsaddled the horses, and loaded them into a trailer for the drive back to Lone Mountain. It seemed important to be clear about my reasons for doing this thing and that probably had something to do with the fact that my daughter would be climbing with me. I don't usually study my motives and I've done my share of impulsive things. Fewer after I became a father; and fewer still as my girls grew older and then grew up. So my thinking was not exactly logical and lucid.

I knew that my plan to climb the Grand, with a guide leading the way, didn't make me Edmund Hillary ("Ed" to his friends) but I didn't think I had to be Chevy Chase, either. I knew that some climbers considered the Grand the "American Matterhorn." Both were beautiful mountains that required some technical climbing (ropes and hardware) if you were going to reach the summit. Amateurs climbed both mountains and a few died trying. Even though accomplished climbers considered it a sort of training wheels mountain, at least one Exum guide had been seriously injured when he fell on the Grand.

I was beginning to feel qualms, I suppose, on the ride down the Gallatin valley, back to Lone Mountain Ranch. The mountains around us had that golden, late afternoon glow and the river sparkled. The setting was conducive to a little brooding.

I knew that friends of mine were saying things like "midlife crisis," about me and thought I was, in some mild sense, a fool. Naturally, I was a little worried, at melancholy moments like this, that they might be right. It wasn't a particularly good time to be a middle-aged man. Grown men—mostly white and middle-aged—were going out into the woods, standing around fires, beating on drums and chanting and talking about "getting in touch with the inner man." I thought it was utter bullshit but wondered if I wasn't guilty of at least acting on the same impulse. A little simulacrum of danger at 50, to trick myself in to believing something that wasn't true and hadn't been for a long time.

But, I told myself, I had wanted to do this for a while now. It just hadn't been possible (or convenient, anyway) until now. And I didn't have to apologize to anyone, even myself, for wanting to do it. For that matter, I didn't have to give myself a headache trying to decipher the imponderable. I *knew* I wanted to climb that mountain. I didn't know why. If I made it, maybe I would find out. But making it would be the real prize. Solving the motive puzzle would be lagniappe.

I somehow resolved all this, in my mind, before we pulled up at Lone Mountain, and it was a big relief. I got out of the truck eager to find Brooke and hear about her day and feeling like I could really go for a beer.

Watching the Clouds

Some confess to having been drawn to climbing by a physical inferiority complex engendered by their failure at school to hit a ball straight and far. —Eric Shipton

The woman at the Exum hut had told me to pray for good weather, but it hadn't been necessary. For a solid week, a vast high-pressure area was parked over Montana, Wyoming, Idaho, and most of the West. We had high blue skies and mild days, thousands of stars and near freezing nights. Every day I looked at the sky and thought, "This can't last."

And it couldn't.

The day we left Lone Mountain, a front came down from the Pacific full of moisture and squall lines. We drove through Yellowstone to get back to Jackson, and the weather deteriorated by the hour. When we stopped at the Exum hut on the way through Moose, the peaks of the Tetons were obscured by thick clouds. It was cold, windy, and raining. We didn't have to be told, but one of the guides who was hanging around the hut told us anyway:

"Doesn't look good for tomorrow. Maybe not for the rest of the week."

Which meant postponing the climb for a year. Brooke had to get back to school and I had to get back to work. There is nothing you can do about the weather. Every outdoorsman knows this and weather has done worse things to climbers than keep them from making a climb. Storms have killed a number of notable climbers, and weather has probably been a factor, at least, in the majority of climbing fatalities. In a sense, Brooke and I were lucky. Better to have the storm blow in before we even started than to be trying for the summit when it came rolling in.

Still . . . for me, the news cast a pall over what was left of the day. Brooke and I shopped for food for the climb—power bars, freeze-dried chicken noodle soup, oatmeal, and tea—and went by an outfitter in Jackson where you could buy anything you needed for climbing or to wear around town if you merely wanted to look like a climber. It was discouraging, looking at the shiny carabiners and expensive, brilliantly colored parkas and feeling like we'd missed our chance.

As we browsed the aisles, I recalled that I'd heard, somewhere, how Yvon Chouinard started the trend for climbing clothes in dazzling colors. Chouinard was a legendary climber in the fifties and sixties. Energetic and innovative, he was a skilled blacksmith who not only made his living that way but also turned out some of his own climbing gear. He was especially famous—in climbing circles—for his pitons, which he hammered out on a forge, that traveled with him in the back of an old truck. Chouinard made enough—barely—to sustain himself and indulge his passion for climbing by selling his hard-steel pitons and working part-time (very) as a private eye. For a while, Chouinard slept in an abandoned incinerator outside of Moose, Wyoming. He ate roadkill and lived to climb.

After his success with something called the Realized Ultimate Reality Piton, or RURP, Chouinard turned his talent for innovation toward one of the basic tools of climbing—the ice ax. He is generally credited with coming up with the curved ax, which enabled ice climbers to make those spectacular ascents of sheer ice faces. He became a small businessman, making climbing hardware and tools, and at some point, he added a few clothes to flesh out the catalog. One of the items of apparel was a pair of heavy canvas climbing pants. A woman who worked for him cut the legs off a pair and looked so good in the resulting shorts that the company began to get requests and added canvas climbing shorts to the product line. They sold and Chouinard soon found himself deep in the clothing business, which he spun off as a separate company. "Patagonia" became one of those labels that people sought not merely for something to wear but also to make a statement. These were outdoor clothes of good quality, intelligent design, and true functionality. They also looked good. And the colors were very jaunty, which was the idea. In the bleak, monochromatic environments where climbers find themselves, a splash of color lifts spirits and improves morale. This was Chouinard's insight, anyway, and it seems, on reflection, inspired.

He made a fortune in business but by all accounts, Chouinard remained a climber, kayaker, angler, surfer, and all-around, self-styled "dirt bag" in spirit. When he was not on the road, he lived in Moose, the site of the incinerator that had once been home.

If Brooke and I knocked on his door, I wondered, would he have something gnomic to say that would lift our spirits?

"Come on, Dad," Brooke said when I suggested it, "get real."

I paid for what we'd bought with my credit card, which got me thinking about the way Chouinard and climbers like him had lived back when they were young. They ate peanut butter and oatmeal and did their financials by counting the money in their pockets. They didn't have credit cards, but then, they didn't worry about a storm in the mountains, either. There was always tomorrow.

We took our goods back to the house in Moose. Ran through the check list one last time and packed our packs, even though it seemed increasingly unlikely that we would need them. The rain was, if anything, heavier and the cloud cover around the peaks of the Tetons was impenetrable. It was getting colder, so in the high altitudes there was probably snow.

I built a fire to warm the house and sat in front of it, drinking wine with Marsha, until dinner time. We had spaghetti (*pasta*, Dad, my girls corrected me), since the carbohydrates were supposed to be good if you were going to be doing something strenuous in the next 24 hours. This, anyway, was the "carbo loading" theory, widely circulated in the health and fitness magazines that Brooke and Marsha read. I wondered if the theory was valid and, if so, was the high carb dinner even necessary? Then I decided it didn't matter, since I was hungry anyway.

We had been together for more than a week now, eating most of our meals together, and we probably should have been tired of each other's company. But it was fun being in the kitchen together, washing lettuce, slicing tomatoes, testing the linguine to see if it was al dente, warming the bread, then sitting down together, once again, to eat.

Hadley played the imp through it all. This is the job of the youngest.

"Pass the bread please, Daddy dearest."

"Don't do it, Dad," Brooke said. "You'll just be playing into her evil power games."

"But I'm hungry."

"Can't you see? It's all a fiendishly clever plot."

"*Please.*"

It was one of those family dinners where you laugh at things no one else would find funny. The long day in the car and my grim obsession with the weather had put everyone on edge, and now the tension was breaking and we were laughing at these old family routines:

"*It's a plot, I tell you. A monstrously clever plot. It's not about pasta at all. It's about power.*"

By the time we got the dishes done and the counters cleaned, Brooke was talking about a game of hearts and promising that she was going to beat me "like a rented mule." It was a phrase that she'd picked up from me, back in my softball coaching days.

"I'll be all over you," Hadley said, "like a cheap suit."

"Like white on rice," Brooke said.

"Do you know these two?" I said to Marsha.

"Never seen them before in my life, Officer."

"Mom."

"Well, then, I guess we'll have to lock them up."

"Your own daughters."

And so on, while I put another couple of logs on the fire and we set up to play cards. I'd more or less forgotten about the mountain. Then, somewhere along about the fifth or sixth hand, and after a lot of loud wailing about the treachery of passing the queen to your own sister, daughter, wife, or husband . . . Brooke cocked her head and said, "I think the rain's stopped, Dad."

We all put down our cards and listened. The only sound was the popping from the lodgepole pine, burning in the fireplace.

"Wouldn't that be *great?*" Brooke said. She plainly wanted it more for me than for herself.

"Yes," I said. "It sure would."

We all went outside. The rain had, in fact, stopped but the wind was still blowing hard and cold.

"Any stars?" I said.

We all looked up at the sky, which was dark and unpromising.

"There's one," Hadley said, and after a while she succeeded in pointing it out to me, very faint and low on the horizon.

"You really do have the eyes," I said.

"Do you think it will clear up?"

"I don't know," I said. "Maybe."

"I think it will," Hadley said and hugged me around the waist.

"I hope so."

"But if it doesn't," she said, "we'll have a birthday party for you down here."

"That would be great."

"But it's going to clear up," she said

"If you say so."

"I do," she said. "And I'm the one who found the star."

▲ ▲ ▲

I knew that it was daylight before I was fully awake—and bright daylight, at that. The kind that seems to penetrate your eyelids. I opened my eyes and saw sunshine, blue sky, and in clear relief, the summit of the Grand.

"Brooke," I shouted, "wake up. It's a go."

We ate oatmeal, filled water bottles, and made one last check of our gear. When I went outside to load the packs into the car, I checked the sky. It was flawlessly clear and blue. The front had moved through, pushed by another big high. Most likely, we would have good weather for a week.

Marsha and Hadley drove us to the Exum hut. It was a quiet ride, which seemed a little odd, after our boisterous evening with the pasta dinner and cutthroat hearts game. Then, on just a little reflection, I realized that it wasn't odd at all; it was perfectly natural. For me and for Brooke, it was simple. The weather was right and we were eager to get going. For Hadley, and especially Marsha, things were not so simple. They were pleased, for our sakes, but they were also apprehensive.

None of us said the words "Be careful" or "Don't worry," but those lines were as much a part of the mood as if they were scripted. Marsha hugged Brooke the same way she had the first time she dropped her off at summer camp.

"Call us when you get down," she said to me and then we

hugged, too. She was apprehensive, I knew that. But she wasn't going to show it and I knew that, too. Marsha hadn't really wanted me to do this. But she hadn't wanted me to leave Brooke out when I decided to do it, either. And once it was clear that we were going to do it, she became our greatest supporter and cheerleader. That was entirely in character. She is, above all, an enthusiast.

Hadley got her hugs in. Then the two of them drove off to join friends for some fishing. Brooke and I shouldered our packs and walked to the Exum hut, where Al Read was waiting to introduce us to our guides.

They were standing outside the hut, arms folded, enjoying the morning sunshine and talking with the nonchalance of major league ballplayers a couple of hours before game time. Both of them were tall and predictably wiry, and they both had the intense eyes, a feature that was beginning to seem universal among climbers and a dead giveaway.

Read made the introductions. Alex Lowe was the younger of the two men; Kim Schmitz, the older. While I may have been a novice climber, I was familiar with both of those names. Lowe had been described, in print, as perhaps the world's finest alpinist: a climber of extraordinary versatility—he did everything from simple rock climbs to Everest—and uncommon strength. I did not know it at the time, but he had just returned from Russia, where he had climbed a 7,000-meter peak as part of an international competition. After Lowe won by more than two hours over the runner up, some other climber in the competition had described the outcome this way: "You had some of the greatest climbers in the world here, and they divided into two groups: everybody else and Alex."

Lowe had a kind of wholesome, attentive face with clean angles and strong bones, and you could imagine him as an actor or even a model. He could have been a thinking man's Tom Cruise. He was, I also learned later, a married man with two children and, by the standards of the climbing community, anyway, a straight arrow.

Kim Schmitz was the other thing. He had been a legend in Yosemite, which was the center of the American climbing universe during the late sixties and early seventies, a place of bold climbs and free spirits where Schmitz made a reputation for himself. Someone familiar with that scene had described him as "a god in the mountains but pure hell in town." He was a part of the climbing elite, known for his first ascents not only in Yosemite but also in the Himalaya and the Karakoram, where he had knocked off the Trango Tower among others.

A few years earlier, when he was in his prime and working as an Exum guide, Schmitz was leading a climb and, for some reason, fell. It was a long fall. Perhaps 80 feet and it is still incomprehensible to climbers who have seen the place where it happened, and imagined what it must have been like, that he lived, that he was not simply killed outright when he hit the ground.

Schmitz survived with hideously broken legs. One of the climbers who reached him first on the rescue later said, "Kim's legs looked like they were about two feet long. The bones had just been driven up into his body. And everything was broken. Just shattered."

Schmitz was operated on many times over several years, and in the course of his long rehabilitation, he struggled with various addictions and depression, understandably enough, but he made it—through his own strong will and the generosity and support of friends, including Yvon Chouinard. He had slain his various demons and was now counseling local people in drug-abuse programs. He was also climbing again (obviously) and other climbers now marveled at his ability to endure what they knew had to be a lot of pain. "There have got to be days," one of them said, "where every move he makes just hurts like hell."

I knew a lot of this story before I ever met Kim Schmitz and learned that he would be taking me and my daughter up the Grand. It was both reassuring and oddly daunting. I felt somehow . . . unworthy.

But we shook hands and exchanged the normal pleasantries. Schmitz had a dazzling smile and slightly sinister good looks and eyes that even the other guides found arresting. "Nobody has eyes like Kim," one of them said. "I mean, they look right through you." He could have played the sophisticated heavy in a movie where Alex Lowe had the guileless leading role.

We were joined by a young couple from Salt Lake City, air traffic controllers on vacation. It was plain from the effortless way they wore their packs that they were capable in the outdoors and that the Grand was not exactly daunting to them.

Brooke and I were raw rookies next to them, while Lowe and Schmitz were from another universe entirely. I felt like an utter pretender in this company and that the proper thing would be to make my apologies and slink off to join other common people somewhere.

We made small talk for a few minutes, with Lowe making an effort to put us at our ease. He was especially gracious toward Brooke, asking her how old she was and what year in school and how she liked the climbing school. He looked at her with those intense, piercing eyes when he asked the questions, and Brooke felt even more ill at ease, mumbling her answers and looking at the ground, obviously feeling the aura of this starlike presence.

Lowe asked if we had certain items that were on the checklist, and we told him we did. I was prepared to unload my pack so he could make a personal inspection of my gear, but he didn't ask. When he finished this casual inventory, he told us to be sure to wear sunscreen and to drink plenty of water and then, with no particular ceremony, not even a "Well, here we go," or words to that effect, we started up a trail into the lodgepole and aspen, on our way to the Grand. It seemed an awfully subdued beginning to something that had been an obsession for such a long time. I felt like I was setting off not on a quest but a picnic.

Which, for the rest of the morning, it could have been. Our packs were light, since we did not have to carry sleeping bags or tents. We would be spending the night at a permanent shelter that Exum had been putting up in what was called the saddle, at 11,600 feet, for years. It had been grandfathered in, by the Park Service, and Exum was the only outfitter with such a permit. There were sleeping bags at the shelter as well as all the necessary cooking and climbing equipment. We carried extra clothes and food for two days. And, perhaps, a book, a camera, or a walkman.

The light load made for easy walking. Somehow, I wound up talking to Alex Lowe about real estate prices. He'd recently bought a house in Bozeman, where he lived with his wife and two young children, one of them still an infant. It was pleasant enough talk. Inoffensive conversation between a couple of guys who were fathers and had mortgages to meet.

Lowe eventually got around to telling me about the climbing competition in Russia and then about an attempt he would soon be making on Everest.

"You work in New York, right?" Lowe said.

"I have," I said. We were still making our way through lodgepole and ponderosa pine, on a gentle incline with lots of switchbacks.

"Then, do you know Bob Pittman?"

"You mean the MTV guy?" I said.

"Yeah, that's him. So you know him?"

"Ah . . . no," I said. "I . . . uh, know who he is."

"Oh," Lowe said, "well, do you know about his wife, Sandy?"

"No," I admitted.

"Well, she's trying to become the first woman to climb the seven summits."

Lowe went on, for a mile or so, explaining about the inspired stunt first pulled off by Dick Bass, owner of Snowbird ski resort, and Frank Wells, who had been president of the Walt Disney company before he was killed in an airplane crash. When both men were in their fifties, not especially experienced mountain climbers, and not even in very good shape, it had occurred to them to become the first people in the world to climb to the highest point on each of the world's seven continents. As their detractors liked to point out, climbing the seven summits was, first of all, a fiscal challenge. Bass and Wells could, indeed, afford to spend more on their project than many great climbers would earn in a lifetime. Also, some of the climbs did not call for a high order of mountaineering skills . . . they were what climbers dismiss as "walk-ups." As a sheer mountaineering challenge, these same detractors liked to point out, climbing the second-highest peak on each of the seven continents would be far tougher. All of which might have been true, but nevertheless, when Bass reached the summit of Everest in 1985, people who had never thought about mountaineering were suddenly inspired to try it. The book, *Seven Summits*, sold a lot of copies and inspired many amateur, well-off climbers to attempt the feat.

One of those, Lowe explained, as he walked along the trail at a kind of effortless lope, was Sandy Hill Pittman, a former magazine editor who had married the founder of MTV. She lived grandly in New York and aimed to be the first woman to climb the seven summits. She had tried Everest once, Lowe explained, but didn't make it. Now she had hired him to be one of her guides on another attempt in the spring.

"Pretty impressive," I said. I was already breathing a little hard. The pace was easy, so it had to be the altitude.

"Yes, it is," Lowe said, somewhat defensively. "Everest is Everest."

"Sure."

"She's not doing any lead climbing or placing any protection. I'll go ahead—me and the other guides—and we'll put in the fixed ropes and then she'll come up on an ascender. But that doesn't cut off any altitude or make it any warmer or mean that she won't have to get herself to the summit."

"For sure," I said. "Good luck. I hope you make it."

They did not, as it turned out. They were turned back by poor conditions that made the threat of avalanches too strong to ignore. Lowe went on to other things, and Pittman continued her own increasingly high-profile quest. She'd sent dispatches to *USA Today* from her unsuccessful attempt with Lowe. On her next try, she would send bulletins, in real time, to her own Web site.

But her successful ascent of Everest in 1996 would be overshadowed by the death of her guide and several other climbers in one of the worst, most celebrated catastrophes in the history of mountaineering, and she would be the heavy in Jon Krakauer's *Into Thin Air*, probably the most compelling book yet written about mountains and climbing.

▲ ▲ ▲

A couple of hours after we had started out, the trail came out of the birches and lodgepole into a deep crease in the mountain and began following the course of a sparkling little stream fed by the melt off the glacier another couple of thousand feet above us.

We stopped and ate lunch where a large, flat boulder jutted out into the stream like nature's patio. I took off my shoes, ate an apple and some cheese, and felt more than ever like I was on a picnic.

This changed when we got back on the trail and as the afternoon wore on. Moving in the boulder field was more difficult than walking on the dirt trail. We began moving up steeper sections so I was no longer erect and admiring the countryside but bent over, looking at the ground ahead of me. Breathing began to feel like work and like you weren't doing it right, somehow. This, of course, was altitude. It was the first time Brooke and I had ever experienced its effects.

The air, as everyone knows, becomes thinner the higher you climb. If you live in New York, travel to Denver on business, and go out jogging, you will feel the effects of the altitude. There are people who have enough difficulty with the 10,000 feet of some Colorado ski resorts that it ruins a vacation. For the milder effects of altitude, you can take an aspirin. High-altitude mountaineers sometimes use stronger, prescription drugs to counter the effects of altitude. Brooke and I took aspirin on a break.

The best way to deal with the effects of altitude is simply to let your body get used to it—to acclimatize. People who live at high altitudes have made the necessary physiological adjustments. Visitors can, too, if they take the time. Climbers have worked out intricate acclimatization schedules (some medical books recommend ascending 1,000 feet a day at altitudes above 12,000 feet), and this is why Everest climbers spend days and weeks at base camp and other low camps before trying for the summit.

That kind of careful acclimatization would be an extravagance here. If you were having serious difficulties with altitude, on a climb like this, then the simple solution would be to turn around, go rest up, and try again another day. We, of course, did not have another day. School started in about a week for Brooke. I had my work. We were not real climbers, barely dilettantes, and if we wanted to do the thing, this would simply have to be the time.

By mid-afternoon, we still had 1,000 feet of altitude and, I guessed, a couple of miles of hiking to go. Lowe and the couple from Salt Lake had moved out ahead, by almost half a mile. Brooke and I were moving slowly up the trail and through the boulder fields, stopping now and then to rest. Kim Schmitz was following us. He walked with ski poles. I assumed at first that he was using them as canes, but after a while it became clear that he did not really need that kind of help. The ski poles helped with balance. Schmitz, who had nothing to prove, would take any small advantage. As we moved up the trail, silent except for our steady panting, we could hear behind us the rhythmic *click, click, click* of the points of Schmitz' ski poles striking rock.

I was breathing hard and the walking was no longer effortless, the way it had been in the morning, back down in the lodgepole. But Brooke was truly laboring. She was not breathing rhythmically but gasping, like a runner who has just finished a race. There was no gate or cadence to her movements. She was struggling and each step was its own ordeal.

It had to be the altitude, I thought, since she had the endurance for this. She ran cross-country at school, training hard and finishing her races even if she didn't win any. We had been running together, in the Vermont hills, right up until we left to come out here. We were both in decent shape. But altitude is something you cannot train for (not at sea level, anyway), and it affects each individual differently.

Brooke, I thought, could be one of those people who are hit hard by altitude, even 10,000 feet. I began to think she might not make it.

▲ ▲ ▲

This brought things to a point I had been afraid of way back when I first announced my plan to try this climb and do it alone. I didn't know how to articulate my concern back then. What I knew was that climbing with your daughter (or son, if I'd had one) changes some of the fundamentals. If Brooke's problems continued and even got worse, there would come a point where the prudent thing would be to quit. Climbers routinely push on, through fatigue and real pain. However, the only treatment for serious altitude conditions (pulmonary edema, cerebral edema, etc.) is to descend and get to a lower altitude. Going higher makes things worse and increases the risks. Not turning around at very high altitude can be fatal.

We weren't that high. Still . . . climbers need clear judgment and if you are a kid, and your dad is along, you might keep going when you shouldn't, just because you don't want to disappoint him. Brooke had, after all, been willing to sit around the house for two hours or more with a broken arm, waiting for her mother to come home and take her to the hospital, so that she wouldn't bother me when I was working. So I could easily imagine her climbing on when her body was signaling her that she should quit.

And, if she did listen to those signals and started back down, then what would I do? Go down with her, I thought, that was the only thing. But it was certain that she would insist that I go on without her and there would be one of those emotional scenes. You get used to them, when you are a parent. But one of the reasons for climbing mountains—heading for the hills— is to put your domestic baggage behind you for a while.

Or, it could have been that she wasn't suffering the effects of altitude any more or less than anyone else and that she was just young and testing the limits of her endurance for the first time. Maybe she just needed some encouragement or a firm push.

"Come on," I might need to say, "you're not tired. Suck it up and keep walking."

I could treat her like a kid, in other words, but I hadn't come here to do that, either. There had already been a slight change in the way we related to each other. It was unavoidable. When you are climbing, you cannot be a kid and expect someone else to take care of you. You have to take care of yourself. And when you do, then you can expect others—even your parents—to stop treating you like a kid.

Kim Schmitz rescued me. He was coming along behind us; not, certainly, because he was slower than we were but because he was the guide and that was where he belonged. We were not likely to get so far ahead of him that he couldn't keep an eye on us.

Brooke had stopped to rest. She was leaning against a boulder, hands on her knees, gasping for breath.

"Don't stop," Schmitz said firmly.

"I have to rest," Brooke said, a little petulant.

"That just makes it harder," Schmitz said. "Find a comfortable pace and keep walking."

I recognized the expression on Brooke's face. Resistance, resentment . . . all the frustrations of a child up against one more adult who just doesn't get it. *Comfortable pace? Give me a freaking break.*

"That's what I do," Schmitz said, giving her a dazzling smile. "It works for me."

Brooke nodded.

"So far, anyway. Worked in the Himalayas and it works in the Tetons."

Brooke nodded again. The truculence leaving her face.

"Actually, you're doing fine. You can slow down the pace a little and we'll still get to camp earlier than I expected."

"Really?"

"Sure. We'll have time to brew up a little tea and enjoy the sunset. It's a real show from 11,000 feet. Makes all this walking seem worth it."

Brooke was breathing normally now. And standing up straight.

Schmitz dug into his pocket and took out a piece of hard candy, wrapped in cellophane.

"Here," he said. "These seem to help."

"Thanks," Brooke said.

"Just find your own rhythm and try to keep it, like dancing."

It never got that easy. Brooke still had to stop and rest, now and then, and I could hear her struggling, trying to take in more of the anemic air. But being told by Kim Schmitz that she was doing fine had given her the boost that she needed. Now she believed that there was a pace that was right for her and that it would carry her smoothly to the saddle. She was still looking for it when we got to camp.

Legends of the Grand

Never a harsh word or a twisted rope. —Glen Exum

A lex Lowe had water boiling and a few minutes after we reached the saddle and the Exum shelter, Brooke and I were sitting on a rock, drinking lemon zinger and looking at the valley where we had been that morning. Everything down there looked very small, like a world in miniature. The shadow of the mountain had already fallen over the valley. We were still in sunshine up here, but a cold wind was moving through the saddle, so Brooke and I put on the fleece jackets we carried in our packs and wrapped our fingers around our mugs for warmth.

"I wonder what Mom and Hads are doing," Brooke said.

I looked at my watch. It was after seven. "Getting ready to go out to dinner, I imagine."

"I hope they aren't worried."

"I believe they've got better things to think about," I said.

"It's so beautiful up here," Brooke said, "that this makes sense to us, you know, while we're doing it. And it feels safe, too. To them down there, it must seem like pure insanity." At that moment, she was still more kid than teenager, worried about worrying her mother.

"You're right," I said. "It probably does."

We finished our tea and walked over to the west face of the saddle and looked out at country that was still bathed in bright yellow sunlight. We had a camera and took some wide-angle shots that would show the rectangular grid imposed on the land by the potato farms. Then we took some telephoto shots of the peaks around us, including the Grand. The summit was hidden but the slopes leading up to it looked steep and forbidding, like the walls to some impregnable castle.

"Think we can do it?" I said.

"I'm not sure," Brooke said. "Not after today, anyway."

"You did fine," I said.

She shook her head and pulled a face; one that said she knew she was being talked to like a kid. *Yeah, sure, Dad.*

"Okay," I said. "But it's supposed to be hard. Remember?"

"That hard?"

"I don't know," I said. "It's my first time, too."

She smiled and nodded.

"Look at it this way," I said, "we did what we had to do today and we're here. No reason we can't do what we have to do tomorrow and get there." I pointed up in the direction of the summit.

"Okay," she said. She still sounded skeptical. But less so.

"You're happy you made it this far, aren't you?"

"Yes."

"Well, then, just imagine how much happier you'll be when you make it the rest of the way."

"Okay," she said again. With more conviction.

We walked back across the saddle to the shelter, with our shoulders hunched and the wind at our backs. Before we reached the other people in our little party, Brooke stopped and said, "Listen, Dad."

"Yes," I said. Her tone was serious; the one she used when she wanted to be sure you treated her like an equal, not like some kid.

"I just wanted to tell you that I really love this," she said.

"Me too."

"So . . . anyway, thanks again for bringing me."

I nodded. It was, I thought, an adult thing to say. And about the best birthday present I could imagine.

▲ ▲ ▲

We joined the others and drank more lemon zinger (we'd been told to avoid the caffeinated stuff, since it causes dehydration) while we watched the mountains around us turn a fiery orange. One peak, especially, seemed to glow like a hot ember. This was called Disappointment Peak, because early climbers tended to get confused about the topography and climb it, thinking they had made the summit of the Grand. Brooke and I shot a roll of 35mm film, mostly of Disappointment Peak, radiant and gold.

Alex Lowe had taken an ice ax and gone off to check out our route for the morning. I learned later that this was typical, restless behavior. Lowe seemed to crave movement and strenuous work. He did 400 pull-ups a day and once, when he was on a long ski trek and trapped in his tent by a storm, he had gone out and found a small crevasse, laid his skis from one edge to the other, then used them as a chinning bar. He told us he was going up to cut steps in the snow and ice if he decided it was necessary, but Kim Schmitz seemed to think that was a cover story, that Lowe just didn't feel like hanging around camp for a sedentary hour or two while it was still daylight.

When he came back down to camp, the light was dying and it was time to eat. Brooke and I had some kind of freeze-dried chicken and noodles, and I was hungry after the work of getting here. While we ate, and the mountains around us fell into shadow, Lowe and Schmitz pointed out the route we would follow in the morning.

"That's Wall Street," Schmitz said, "just above that big dark stain on the rock."

We looked until we were sure we were looking at the feature he was talking about. Wall Street was what the climbers called a wide ledge that traversed the mountain at a slight angle.

"It's the ledge Glen Exum took," Lowe said. "And when he got to the end, he took a big chance."

The name Exum is beyond famous in American climbing circles. It is durable and legendary. The guide service, which employed Schmitz, Lowe, Pratt, and so many other great climbers, once belonged to him and still bears his name. Dozens of elite climbers worked for him and admired and respected him with an intensity that was close to reverent. Yvon Chouinard wrote of Exum: "Glen's life is the story of a man who exemplifies Saint-Exupery's 'Freedom is acceptance of responsibility.' Glen has always known that his role in life is to lead men."

The route we would be taking in the morning, on our attempt to reach the summit of the Grand, is called the Exum route, and it is the source of the Glen Exum legend. Exum, who had never climbed before, pioneered the route on July 15, 1931. He was wearing a pair of cleated football shoes that had been loaned to him by Paul Petzoldt, an experienced climber and Exum's friend. Petzoldt had two clients and wanted to take them to the summit by the typical route. He told Exum to take a look at a ledge. "If you think it will go, why, go, and we'll meet you at the top," Petzoldt said, "and if you don't think it will go, call me and we'll wait for you."

When Exum called, Petzoldt couldn't hear him. So Exum went back out on the ledge, returned, then went back out again. Seven times. Finally, from a point where the ledge narrowed to nothingness, with the mountain falling away some 2,000 feet below him, he saw that if he jumped across a gap of a few feet, he would reach some handholds on a ridge that appeared to lead straight on up to the summit. He was alone and there was no one belaying him, so if he missed the jump, he would fall and die.

Petzoldt, the experienced climber, was astounded to find Exum waiting at the summit when he got there. He tried the route later but used a rope to lasso a bolder on the other side of the gap and belay himself before he jumped.

"Nowhere in the history of mountaineering has anyone received as much acclaim and notoriety for 20 feet of climbing as Glen did," according to Jack Durrance, another celebrated American climber.

Exum and Petzoldt went on to become the established guides in the Tetons, with Exum eventually taking over the business entirely and running it for more than 20 years before selling to Al Read and three of his other senior guides. He made some 300 ascents of the Grand and while the first was legendary, you could make a case that the last was truly sublime.

It took place on July 15, 1981, on the precise anniversary of the first climb and that wonderfully bold move from Wall Street to what became "the Exum ridge." Glen Exum was 70 years old and he was still recovering from surgery for cancers of the prostate and colon. He was not sure that he would be strong enough to make the climb. "If I was going to climb it," he said, "I wanted to climb it in style, without assistance."

When it became clear that he would be able to climb according to his own demanding standards, the word went out that the thing was on and Exum's many climbing friends began calling, saying they wanted to be included.

At 5:00 A.M. on the fiftieth anniversary of his celebrated climb, Exum left the hut in the lower saddle, where we would be sleeping tonight, and headed for the summit. There were thirty people behind him. This included two television crews and 13 of Exum's guides, past and present. The mood was as festive as a Mardi Gras parade.

Some of Exum's close friends and climbing buddies were not among the happy group, most conspicuously Willi Unsold, who had been killed two years earlier in an avalanche on Mount Ranier. Unsold, who had lost nine toes in the extraordinary 1963 high-altitude bivouac on Everest, had been one of Exum's closest friends, as well as one of his guides. They had made the fortieth-anniversary climb together, and when they reached the end of Wall Street, the point of Exum's leap, Unsold had said a prayer that moved Exum deeply then and which he wanted, somehow, to replicate on this occasion, the fiftieth anniversary of that first climb and also, no doubt, the last time he would ever climb the Grand.

A friend agreed to attempt a prayer appropriate to the occasion, and when the band of climbers reached the end of Wall Street, they all removed caps, bowed heads, and listened to the words:

"Almighty Father, hear our prayer! Watch over and protect us, and if it be Thy will, grant us success as we celebrate a long-ago historic event in the life of Thy servant, Glenn; especially we commemorate his life, his leadership, teachings, principles, and example which have turned countless persons now scattered across Your beautiful earth in the direction of goodness and strength. Watch over him we pray, as this small group and countless others accord him the recognition, respect, honor, and love which he has so fully earned and so richly deserves. While your eye is on the sparrow, Lord, let it be on the eagle here with us today! And, Lord, somewhere in Your glorious realm there labors a friend of ours, doubtless striving to improve the lot of angels as he strove to improve the lot of men here on earth. Free Willi, we pray, from his heavenly duties and let him roam with us today in the spirit, as he would have, but for Thy will, in person. Each of us thanks You in his day's activities and to share the companionship of this special group of men. In Thy blessed name we pray. Amen."

Exum later said, "Something happened to me at that moment and I felt that I had wings on my feet as I flowed across the end of Wall Street, passed the big boulder, and reached the base of the ridge. I threw the rope across the big rock, placed myself into position, and shouted to my son Ed, "On belay!""

He led the climb, all the way to the summit, with people changing places on the rope with him, so they (and he) could say that they had made this climb together. Al Read climbed one pitch called the Golden Staircase with Exum, and Chouinard shared his rope on the "Friction Pitch."

At the summit, Exum wept when he was presented with a gold-plated Chouinard ice ax and other mementos. There was champagne, chilled in the snow, waiting when the climbers returned to the saddle. It was Exum's kind of climb:

"Never a cross word or a twisted rope."

▲ ▲ ▲

I like that story as much as any climbing story I know. I'd heard part of it from Al Read, one afternoon at the hut down in the valley, and we heard more of it that night, from Lowe and Schmitz. I learned the entire story, a few years later, from a privately published book about the life of Glen Exum. That story struck me, I suppose, because it stood for what I hoped Brooke and I would "learn" in our slight experience in climbing. There was already plenty of exhibitionism and ugly competitiveness in climbing, which seemed especially unfortunate, since you could find those things just about anywhere in the culture. But that spirit seemed so manifestly wrong for the mountains; so contrary to the whole impulse of climbing, which in the end is just an extension of the old childish urge to climb a tree so high that you wind up scaring yourself and daring yourself to go on. There is no *point,* or *objective,* to climbing mountains, which is the beauty of it and why doing it with the kind of style and grace Exum brought to the pursuit seems so important and so wonderful. And probably why the ambitions of climbers like Sandy Pittman (whose lot, it seems, is to stand in for a whole generation of villains) put so many people's teeth on edge.

I remembered, while listening to Alex Lowe talk about Glen Exum's splendid climb, how my girls had once asked me, when they were still little and capable of a question a minute, nonstop for an hour, "Why do people build statues?"

"Same reason they build steeples on churches," I said. (This wasn't original. I'd gotten it from my brother.)

"But why is that?"

"Same reason they play music."

"But *why?*"

"Well, I suppose it's because they can. And because they feel good about having done it."

Which is a longer, inelegant paraphrase of Mallory's immortal line. Climbing is pointless but very serious business.

Brooke and I weren't ever going to fire the competitive envies of the climbing community with any first ascents. We would always be going where others had been first, and we would probably always be on a rope below someone who could get there better. But maybe by going there together we might feel a little hint of the mood that must have been in the air on that fiftieth-anniversary climb with its camaraderie, prayers, and champagne. Maybe we would share a little of the joy that comes with doing the pointless, impractical things with just a little bit of style.

Anyway... it seemed like a best possible impulse to be feeding on one's fiftieth birthday, and by now it *was* my birthday, Eastern Daylight Time.

"Good night, Brooke," I said when we were inside the hut, zipped into our sleeping bags. "And thanks for coming."

"Good night, Dad," she said. "And thanks for bringing me."

Grand Conclusion

It was as if I were the last survivor of the Universe, and saw its corpse stretched under my feet.

—H-B. de Saussure

Somewhere in the deep part of the night, I woke with a full bladder and made my way to the door of the hut, taking care not to step on any sleeping climbers. It was very cold outside—in the twenties, I guessed—and unusually still, without even a slight current of air moving through the saddle. I walked tentatively across to the western side. Schmitz had told us to be sure, always, to pee into Idaho.

I didn't usually wake up in the middle of the night like this, so now that I was fully and officially qualified for membership in the AARP, I allowed myself to wonder: was it prostate or was it too much lemon zinger? I decided not to worry about it and stood braced on a ledge of wide, flat rock while I took care of business. The sky was full of stars, hundreds of them, spread chaotically across a vast, imponderable blackness. It was a sky to make you feel infinitesimally small and utterly free and looking at it too long would give you a profound sense of vertigo. Standing there, on the side of a mountain in my ski underwear, flowing onto the rocks, I had one of those moments when you understand, with absolute lucidity, the modern, philosophical notion of absurdity.

▲ ▲ ▲

I was shuddering from the cold by the time I got back to the hut, where I burrowed deeply into my sleeping bag and zipped it up to my chin.

I woke up a couple of hours later, when Lowe struck a match and lit the stove to boil water. It was four o'clock. We had an hour to get dressed and eat some breakfast. We would be starting out for the summit at five.

The stove threw some light and when Lowe lit a small lantern, it was bright enough to look around the interior of the hut and make out shapes, and even faces, indistinctly. Brooke was still asleep, with the bag zipped up to her neck and in the weak light, the blonde hair surrounding her face looked like an antique picture frame. I lay there, with my head propped on my elbow, watching her for a minute or two. Brooke opened her eyes, blinked once or twice as though she was making sure of where, exactly, she was. When she saw me and saw that I was awake, she said, "Happy birthday."

Hard to imagine a better present.

▲ ▲ ▲

We dressed. Ate some gluey instant oatmeal, not so much because we were hungry but because we knew we had to, then followed Alex out of the saddle and across a boulder field, toward the ledge, Wall Street, that we would take up to the Exum ridge and then, with luck, the summit.

But the boulder field was hard going, especially in the dark. Almost right away Brooke was struggling and gasping for air, the way she had been in the afternoon, on the way to the saddle. She stopped to rest and Lowe told her she had to keep moving.

"I can't," she said. "I can't do it."

"Sure you can," Lowe said cheerfully. "Just keep walking."

Brooke made a sound, between a sob and a sigh, and started back up through the boulder field. I found myself thinking that the big thing to do—my gift to her on my birthday—would be to say, "The hell with it. Who needs this?" and lead her back down the mountain.

We still had 500 or 600 yards of the boulder field to get through before we even began the real climbing. And that would have to be the hard part, I thought. Certainly harder than this, which was just walking. I was breathing hard, but nothing like Brooke. I tried to slow my already slow pace, to think of myself as handling a boat and using only enough power to keep underway. Maybe at a little slower pace, she would do better. What, after all, was the hurry?

For the next hour or so, as we moved through the boulder field in the dark and I listened to Brooke's labored breathing and the urgings of Lowe as he told her, firmly but without condescending, to keep moving, this whole scheme of mine began to seem like a foolish, adolescent stunt, and I kicked myself as an unfeeling fool for putting my little girl through it.

This was a long, long way from the mood of the evening before, when we were listening to the tales of Glen Exum and his glorious climbs and a clear example of something I was to learn about climbing. In the mountains, emotions are like the weather: highly unpredictable and tending to extremes. Which could explain why the real climbers I'd met—Rowell, Read, Lowe, Schmitz—seemed to keep the emotional thermostat turned down.

I had stopped thinking about the summit and was merely walking and mentally composing my speech to persuade Brooke to quit and let me go back to the saddle with her, when

Lowe said, "Okay, we're at the end of Wall Street. This is where we rope up."

We were finally climbing.

▲ ▲ ▲

We were crowded onto the thin ledge, at the point where Lowe would make a move onto the Exum ridge and Schmitz would belay him. With modern equipment, especially the sticky rubber shoes, you didn't have to leap across the way Exum had. With the technique called smearing, where you simply stick yourself to the rock like a fly, using the sticky soles of your shoes for traction, you could make the move. While Lowe and Schmitz were getting set up, I looked around and tried, for the first time, to take it all in.

For 20 minutes or so, it had been bright enough that we could see. But now the sun was actually showing above the horizon, still cool enough that you could look at it. The rock around us glowed orange and even the air seem slightly tinted by this early light. Looking straight out, I could see the flat, dun-colored prairie country expanding out beyond Jackson. And then, looking straight down, I saw nothing for 1,500 or 2,000 feet. At the bottom of this void, the glacier glittered in the early light. This was what climbers call exposure. It means that there is nothing below you. Only air.

We had been told to expect it. And I had anticipated that my first experience with a lot of exposure would be a test of some kind. At the worst, I thought, I would freeze up, lose all my resolve and determination, and tell the guides I wanted to go back down. But the exposure did not affect me that way at all. It was, in fact, bracing. I looked down, actually leaning out a little from the rock, and I felt a rush, a pump, an undeniable thrill at being right where I was. Exposed.

"Is that awesome or what?" Brooke said. She was in front of me, looking at the same things I was seeing, and feeling the same thing I was feeling.

Lowe went across the gap, effortlessly, like it was on flat ground. He took a belay position and called for the next climber. The couple from Salt Lake followed Lowe across and then it was Brooke's turn.

I watched. There was nothing else I could do unless I wanted to look away or close my eyes and that would have been impossible. The rational part of me knew that I had nothing to worry about; she was belayed by the finest mountain climber in the world and it was a fairly easy move. Still, she was my little girl and it was 2,000 feet down to the glacier's sparkling white surface.

Brooke put her hands over her head, spread them wide for balance, then plastered her feet to the rock. She moved with conviction and was across easily and quickly, like she had been doing this all her life. I exhaled. Then I stepped forward and followed her.

Once we were all on the Exum ridge, Schmitz and his climbers moved out ahead of us. We followed them up a piece of moderately angled rock. It was easy climbing. Not only was it not especially steep, it also had plenty of cracks and ledges for hand and foot holds. It would have been a cinch at the climbing school. The exposure made it more demanding.

▲ ▲ ▲

The route up the Exum ridge to the summit of the Grand takes climbers through a series of pitches. You climb belayed, up a pitch, and then you walk a piece of relatively flat ground, carrying the rope in coils, until you reach the next pitch where a belay is required. Exum guides don't require a belay anywhere on the mountain. Most of them don't take a belay from the clients because it would slow them down and might lead to bigger problems. An inattentive client might tighten up on the rope just when the guide is making a move. You can get pulled off the rock that way. Nobody is sure, but some people believe that this is what happened when Kim Schmitz took his terrible fall.

Alex Lowe did not have to take a belay on our climb, but he did. Probably because he knew I was a writer and felt it might not look good in print that he was climbing unprotected with clients. Or maybe he was doing Brooke a favor. For the rest of her life, she could tell people that she'd belayed Alex Lowe in the Tetons.

If taking a belay slowed Lowe down, he was still moving quickly, with a kind of native urgency that was dramatic to watch. When he coiled a rope, his hands moved so rapidly that they seemed a blur. He sorted through the hardware on his sling—carabiners, friends, and figure eights—like a gambler shuffling a deck of cards, his fingers absolutely intimate with the things they touched. And when he started up the rock, he'd make one move, then another, and in less time than seemed humanly possible, he was up the pitch.

He had a way of urging us on, a kind of youthful, persuasive, ingenuous enthusiasm that was just about irresistible.

"We're doing great, aren't we," he would say, with the rope flying through his hands as he recoiled it. He smiled widely enough that you could see half the dazzling white teeth in his mouth and then he would say, "What a great morning, huh? Isn't this just the greatest thing in the world?"

Brooke and I would agree, passionately, that yes, indeed, this was just the greatest thing in the world. You would say it whether you believed it or not because you just couldn't stand to disappoint Alex Lowe by throwing water on his wonderfully uncomplicated enthusiasm. Alex Lowe, you could be sure, never had to wonder why people climbed mountains. For him, a more interesting, and even imponderable question would be—why anyone *didn't* climb mountains.

We did not rest and we did not stop to admire the view or to reflect on what we had already accomplished. We kept moving.

Somebody was always climbing. Lowe would start up a pitch and we would quickly lose sight of him, but we would know that he was moving by the rope that he pulled along behind him, fast enough that Brooke had to work hard to keep feeding him slack. After a few minutes, the rope would stop paying out, then Lowe would holler down, "Off belay." This meant he had anchored himself in and no longer needed Brooke to protect him. She would drop the rope and shout up, "Belay off."

The rope to her harness would come tight and Brooke would shout, "That's me."

"On belay," Lowe would shout.

"Climbing," Brooke would shout back and start up. She moved with confidence and, if I hadn't watched Lowe, I would have thought she was moving quickly. She wasn't, of course, but to her father, who was very proud, she looked strong and confident. And up here, over 12,000 feet high, I was the only one watching.

▲ ▲ ▲

Each pitch had a name and each was a little different in character, requiring a little something different from the novice climber. The first pitch, after Wall Street, was the Golden Staircase, where the rock is flecked with crystal that does, actually, turn gold in the early morning light. Then, after some walking, you come to the Wind Tunnel. There was ice on the rock here, and it felt cold and forbidding. But the moves were not hard and we were up fairly quickly.

By now, the sun was well above the horizon. The air was bright, clear, and cold. There were no clouds in the intensely blue sky and only the slightest suggestion of wind. It was a day to match Alex Lowe's mood. Brooke and I were struggling with the meager air, but we were still confident when we reached the Friction Pitch, the most difficult piece of the climb.

It wasn't as steep as some of what we had climbed down in

the valley. But, again, there was a lot of exposure. We were high on the mountain now, and any sense that we were somehow just playing at it had vanished. We might not have been experienced climbers but we were certainly climbing. This was not virtual reality.

On the Friction Pitch, you use the sticky rubber on your shoes to make your most secure contact with the rock because the holds are small and, in a few places, nonexistent. So you lean back from the rock—that counterintuitive thing—to drive your weight over your feet, and you use your hands to grab what you can find or merely place them flat on the rock for balance.

After Lowe was up and in a secure position, he called down to Brooke that she was on belay. I watched her as long as I could, until she was out of sight. She hadn't made the most difficult section of the pitch, yet, but she looked good. She seemed to be getting stronger the higher we got on the mountain and the more challenging the climbing became. She was not the same person, up here, that she had been down in the boulder field.

For several minutes, the rope moved sporadically and slowly before it stopped moving entirely. Then the last few feet of slack was pulled briskly out of my hands. When the rope was tight to my harness, I called up, "That's me."

Brooke answered, instead of Lowe. Her voice was thin but I could make it out.

"On belay," she said.

"Climbing," I shouted back.

"Climb on."

Lowe had told us that the easy way to handle the Friction Pitch was to stay left. "You've got a pretty wide crack out there that you can use," he said. "But if you aren't careful, you'll get pushed out to the right. It's harder out there."

I started up, looking for the next hold and when I found one, taking it. I tried to make myself look ahead, to plan the next three or four moves, to anticipate and visualize. Good climbers can study the rock and pick out a line and find a route before they ever make a move. But I was the rankest kind of novice and I took what the rock would give me. It was a desperate, profligate approach where you don't pass up a good hold now for considerations about the future. A bird in the hand, and so forth.

The holds I found took me on a line away from the wide, useful crack and out to the right, onto more exposed, polished rock where the holds became small rounded knobs. By the time I realized my mistake, and remembered what Lowe had told us about staying left, I was stuck, way out on a steep, smooth wall of rock, with no holds to speak of. I was out of moves and just about out of ideas.

I looked up to a ledge, 20 or 30 feet above me, into the face of my daughter who was sitting braced, with the rope around her waist, holding me on belay. Some kind of aperture opened in my mind at that moment, creating an indelible mental image of the scene with the words, "Belayed by Brooke," formed somewhere, almost like a caption.

I suppose it is what every father feels when it occurs to him, in a moment of clarity, that his children are his anchor.

▲ ▲ ▲

I did not have time to dwell on the insight. I needed to make something happen.

"Are you okay?" Brooke said.

"Couldn't be better," I answered.

"You got out to the right," Lowe said. "Look for a hold just about at your right knee."

It was very small, the size of my thumb or smaller. But it was all that I had to work with. I had to try it and . . . trust the belay.

"Once you've started," Lowe said, "just keep moving on up. Don't stop."

I made the move and one hand found something. Holds appeared and, when they didn't, the sticky rubber on my shoes and my own momentum were enough to keep me on the mountain and going up.

When I got to a spot just below the ledge where there were big holds and I could stop to rest, Lowe said, "You just did the Friction Pitch the hard way. Congratulations."

"Way to go, Dad," Brooke said.

As birthdays go, I thought, this one was shaping up into something really special.

▲ ▲ ▲

There wasn't much real climbing left, after the Friction Pitch. We walked to a little couloir and then made the moves up the dihedral, or open-book crack, that is called Unsold's Lieback. None of this seemed especially hard and Brooke and I were now smiling at each other and saying the obvious things about the view, which was, in truth, pretty impressive. If you looked over the toes of your boots, the world just fell away and you saw the tops of mountains, looking insignificant now, that had appeared huge and formidable when you had stared up at them from the valley. Looking down like that on those mountains, gave you a feeling of . . . "what?" I thought. It isn't superiority; though the term "conquest" appears a lot in the literature of climbing. But it wasn't quite that.

Whatever the correct term, I was not going to come up with it in my oxygen-starved state and not with Alex Lowe urging us along, to the summit. Brooke and I were content with the commonplace, well-used terms. "Fantastic" seemed perfect and all-purpose.

We were on the ridge just below the summit now, the one that looks, from the valley, like the mountain's shoulder. We had to climb a little chimney and make a kind of stemming move across a small bulge. After that, we carried our ropes in coils and walked across a couple of snowfields and, without being quite prepared for it, arrived at the summit of the Grand.

Coming Down

And now that I have climbed and won this height, I must tread downward through the sloping shade And travel the bewildered tracks till night. —D. G. Rossetti

It was about nine in the morning. Kim Schmitz and the couple from Salt Lake were stretched out on the summit rocks, enjoying the sun, which was well up now and very warm. The sky was blue and flawless. We would look north into Yellowstone Park and see, more than fifty miles away, the water vapor from Old Faithful when it erupted. I took some pictures of Brooke. She took some of me. Alex Lowe used my camera to take some of both of us. I thanked him for getting us up the mountain and he said we'd done fine. We drank some water and ate some raisins. Fifteen or twenty minutes after reaching the summit, we started down.

It was not an easy climb, back down to the saddle. It is a commonplace in the literature of climbing that coming down can be more dangerous than going up. Climbers are tired and have lost their edge. Often they are hurrying to beat sunset or the arrival of bad weather, which was not a problem in our case but has been the cause of many climbing accidents.

We made a long rappel, cutting off a lot of tedious climbing. Rappelling had seemed dramatic in the valley. Here, it was something to be grateful for, like an elevator when you really don't feel like taking the stairs. We reached the boulder field around noon and the saddle a little later. I was hungry and tired, which was natural enough. But there was something else, a letdown maybe, an abiding sense of anticlimax.

We ate lunch at the hut. Schmitz had run out of water to boil and I asked if I could walk down to the spring, a couple of hundred yards away, and fill the empty jerry can for him.

"We're not supposed to ask the clients for help," he said.

"I won't tell," I said.

He shrugged and I carried the empty plastic container down the mountain to a place where I could fill it with glacier melt. I had to stop and rest a couple of times on the way back up. My chest was burning and I felt like I could not get enough air. I had carried five-gallon containers before but never one that felt this heavy. It was, I realized, the altitude.

We ate some lunch, then started down the mountain. We were strung out across the trail fairly quickly. Lowe moved as fast going down as he had coming up. And Brooke continued to gain strength. My knees ached and I fell behind.

I was alone in the glacier moraine, picking my way from boulder to boulder. The trail disappeared entirely from time to time so you simply looked for the most efficient way down the hill. Eventually, a piece of the trail would reappear and you could follow it for a while. Then it was back into a maze of rock with no direct line and no path. You merely worked your way down with no way of establishing any kind of rhythm. It was tedious going.

But you had to pay attention, just enough that it was impossible to think about anything else. You couldn't wonder about what had happened to someone you'd suddenly remembered from high school or ponder some old disappointment and imagine how things could have turned out differently, the way you can when you are walking a grooved trail on your way to the evening's campsite.

I lost track of time and of just about everything except the work of stepping up to this flat rock instead of down to that round one. Brooke was somewhere up ahead, but I had lost sight of her. My guide, Lowe, could easily be back at the Exum hut, the way he was moving.

I set my own pace and I picked my own route. I stopped, once or twice, to rest and drink some water and adjust my pack. It seemed to take as long getting down through the scree as it had going up through it. And this was the obligatory part. Going up, you can quit anytime. Just turn around and say the hell with it. But once you are up, you have to get down. And, perhaps because there is no element of choice involved, going down just seems like drudgery. There is, I suppose, some sort of crucial insight there; some sliver of wisdom about life. But I wasn't up to formulating it. I just kept walking and tried to ignore the grinding sensation in my knees.

I finally came out of the boulder field and found the trail leading into the lodgepole and birch woods below. Brooke had stopped where the trail went into the trees. She was waiting for me and she waved when she saw me. I waved back. I'd known she would be somewhere up ahead, but I was still so happy to see her that it could have been a surprise meeting after a long absence.

I gave her an awkward hug when I reached her. Hugging is hard when you are wearing a pack.

"How are you doing?" I asked, because I was the dad. She probably should have asked the question, since I was the one who had fallen behind. On the way up, she had struggled. Now I was slow.

"Great," she said, and in truth, she looked and sounded fresh. A lot fresher than I felt. "But you know what?"

"What's that?" I said.

"I kept thinking, all the way down to here, that I couldn't believe I ever made it all the way up."

"It was a hike," I said. "No question about it. And all that, just to spend 15 minutes on the summit."

"It was worth it," she said firmly.

"You really feel that way?"

"For sure," she said. "This is the coolest thing I've ever done. I still can't believe I did it."

I liked hearing that and I smiled.

"Dad, I really appreciate your bringing me."

"It was great for me," I said.

"And I'm so glad you made me keep going," she said. "I'm sorry I wimped out like that."

"You didn't wimp out."

"Yeah, I did," she said. "But you got me past it. You and Alex and Kim."

"Well . . ."

"No," she said, "you did, really. Get used to it."

I certainly wasn't used to being talked to like this by my daughter. I didn't know what to say.

"Anyway, thank you. You're the best."

Well, the presents just kept rolling in, here on my birthday, and we hadn't even had the party yet.

▲ ▲ ▲

We walked together, talking about this and that, with me doing more listening than talking, and when we had gone a ways into the trees, we met up with Lowe, who was waiting for us at the head of one of the switchbacks.

"Sorry you had to wait," I said.

He smiled. Then his expression changed and he said, "Something wrong?"

"No," I said. "Why?"

"You're limping."

"Oh," I said, "that's just my knees."

"What's wrong with them?"

"They're old."

He smiled again. There was a lot to admire about Alex Lowe, I thought. Not least his capacity for enjoying things. Big climbs, small jokes, and all sorts of things in between.

"Well," he said, "it isn't far now. Just take it easy and we'll be there in an hour."

"I'm in no hurry," I said.

Lowe walked with me a while. He might have imagined that in my broken-down state, I could use the company. I was fine but I did enjoy talking with him. We talked about kids. His were very young.

"Enjoy them while you can," I said.

"Yeah," Lowe said. "They say it goes fast."

"You won't believe how fast. One day you're watching them take the first step and then"—I nodded here in the direction of Brooke, who had moved out ahead of us on the trail—"you've got one of those."

"She's a good kid," Lowe said, almost as though he were trying to reassure me.

"I know," I said. "But she grew up on me."

The conversation went on, in the usual way, with neither of us saying anything especially revealing or personal. But we both enjoyed talking about our kids and, I suppose, took the business of being a father more seriously than some might. I wasn't anything special in the world but Alex Lowe was a master of his particular universe and a celebrity within it. That world would have given him a pass if he hadn't really connected with his kids. But that wasn't the case. He plainly liked thinking of himself as a dad.

I was still feeling some kind of glow after the climb. It had been, I realized, much more than just a stunt, something that I'd done on a private dare, like bungee jumping, and that I would quickly forget. I had enjoyed that climb in a profound way and it had been a lot more than fun to me. I hadn't found the language yet to articulate why the climb had affected me so strongly—that would come later. For now, it was sufficient for me to realize that it had and to wonder—what if I had tried climbing when I was younger?

I wasn't flattering myself, the way a lot of men do, thinking that if I'd just had the coaching or the opportunities or the breaks, I could have been . . . and here you fill in the blanks. Quarterback, fighter pilot, movie star, mountain climber. I certainly wouldn't have become an Alex Lowe or Kim Schmitz and would have probably been lucky to wind up like the man Brooke and I met on the first day of climbing school, in the rain, under the eaves. Another nomad, roaming the countryside in a Volkswagen bus, searching for righteous rock.

It could have happened that way. I'd tried life as a free spirit and the only thing missing had been the climbing. Eventually I had become a married man and father, and sometimes, when it seemed like that meant the end of that part of life that made the nerve ends sing and let you forget about money and appointments, I had moments when I regretted the way it turned out. Then felt guilty for it and wondered if other men, better men and better fathers than I, ever had weak moments like that. Suspected that even they did.

I wondered, as I walked and chatted with him, if Alex Lowe ever had his version of that kind of moment. He, of course, would never think that if it hadn't been for the kids, he would be in the mountains. He would be in the mountains, in spite of the kids. His regrets, then, if he experienced any, would be on the day when he was on his way to the Himalayas to guide Sandy Pittman up Everest and earn the money to pay that mortgage we had talked about on the way up the Grand, a day earlier. Money that he might regret having to earn.

But regrets inevitably fall under the domain of James Burnham's great rule: "Where there is no solution, there is no problem." Pointless to dwell on them and anyway, I thought, I had climbed my mountain today and done it with my daughter. Had, at 50, found some way to indulge that side of my nature and done it without denying the other side. Which was a neat trick. What I wanted to do now was get down, the rest of the way, off this mountain and catch up with Marsha and Hadley, the rest of my little family. I knew that once we were all back together, there would be some kind of celebration with cake, ice cream, and champagne. I looked forward to that intensely, to our all being together for a while. I felt it even more keenly when I shook hands with Lowe at the end of the trail and watched him move off to embrace his wife then pick his toddler up and swing him over his head. Dad was home, after a hard day on the job, and everyone was glad to see him. What could be nicer?

Celebrations

Beyond the border and under the lark full cloud
There could I marvel my birthday —Dylan Thomas

Brooke and I found the car that Marsha and Hadley had left for us in the parking lot with the keys in the gas cap, where they had told us to look. They had gone with a friend, to his place a couple of hours south of Jackson. We were supposed to join them tonight. In the morning we were all going for a two-day float on the South Fork of the Snake, where the fishing was said to be first-rate. But first Brooke and I had to stop by the place where we were staying in Moose to change. I was looking forward to a hot shower and clean clothes.

When we got to that house, I made two calls. One to my mother, down in Florida, to tell her we had made it up and down the mountain safely. She'd thought this climb was a bad idea, all along, especially where her granddaughter was concerned, so she was relieved and she thanked me for the flowers that had come that morning. It was something I'd started doing a few years earlier. Every year, on my birthday, I sent her a dozen roses.

Then I called the number where Marsha was staying. She was out so I left a short message: "We made it."

A few minutes later, Brooke and I were on the road. It was a long, quiet ride. We were both tired. The day had begun at four o'clock when Alex Lowe struck that match. A long day and also exhausting. We may have worked hard for several weeks to get in shape, but we had still been stretched by the climb. Brooke had told me that it was the hardest thing, by far, that she had ever done. I'd done harder things, as a soldier, but I'd been young and they didn't give you any choice. After the climb, I was tired and sore. My knees ached. The rest of my body was simply weary. We stopped at a convenience place for coffee. I was afraid of falling asleep at the wheel.

Brooke and I did not talk much on the drive, even after we had some caffeine inside us, and this was unusual. She was what they call a verbal kid. When she came home from the movies and you asked her how it had been, she did not simply say "Okay," or "Dumb," or reply with some other monosyllabic critique. She told you everything about the movie. When she was away and called home, the conversations could last an hour or more.

But as we headed down the valley of the Snake River this evening, she was quiet. Not silent or brooding, exactly. Just quiet. We each made a few weak attempts at getting some kind of conversation going, but none of them went anywhere. We were both content to ride along in the fading light, drinking our coffee and nursing our private thoughts.

My thoughts, in fact, were about her. I wondered what she was thinking. She was 15 years old and this meant that most of her life was still an unknown. Unlike, for instance, mine.

I tried to remember back to when I was her age, when my future was still vastly larger than my past, when there was all that possibility out there. It could seem either troubling or purely thrilling, depending on your mood and what kind of day you'd had. I remembered that, and I suspected that it was the same for Brooke, even though youth and, for that matter, all of life had gotten harder since I was her age. I wanted to help, even if it was in simply finding a way to think about imponderable things, but I knew I couldn't.

▲ ▲ ▲

We celebrated at the Silver Spring Lodge outside of Afton, Wyoming. Celebrated my birthday and a successful climb. It was a small, private celebration. The four of us—Marsha, Brooke, Hadley, and me—and our old friend from back in Vermont, Leigh Perkins, recently retired as CEO of Orvis. Perkins is an uncommonly enthusiastic man who pursues his sports with a kind of verve and dedication I admire. He never missed a chance to go fly-fishing or bird hunting, and when he went, he went all out, with the idea that he was going to have a good time even if he didn't catch or kill anything. When he was in college in the fifties, his roommate had been his bird dog, and one weekend he went out grouse hunting thinking that he felt so bad because he had stayed up so late the night before at a fraternity party. When he didn't feel any better—felt worse, in fact—after a couple of hours in the field, he decided that he was suffering from something more serious than the usual Saturday morning hangover. Maybe, he thought, he had the flu. Finally, he couldn't stand up any longer. He wound up crawling back to his car, and when he made it back to the school infirmary, his condition was quickly diagnosed. He had polio.

He was sent to the state hospital and put in a ward with other young polio victims, some of whom were in iron lungs. He recovered with no lasting effects—except, perhaps, a greater appetite for life. I suspect he would go out into the field today, feeling the same way he had then and stay out again until he couldn't stand up. He would have made a good mountain climber.

"By God," he said when he saw Brooke and me, "you look

great. Both of you. I had no idea mountain climbing was so healthy. You look like you're glowing."

Like a lot of my friends, Perkins had been skeptical about this climbing business. He didn't see the point. Not as long as there was a trout stream anywhere in the world that he hadn't yet fished. But he liked the idea that if I was doing it at all, I was doing it with Brooke.

He congratulated us lavishly.

So did Marsha and Hadley, who said, "You two are really neat. I've got the coolest sister and dad of anyone."

I asked her if she was ready to try it.

"Nope," she said. "That's something for you and Brooke."

I felt a little spasm of remorse. She had been left out, even though it was by choice. Hadley seemed sanguine, but then, she already knew that there are harder things in life than climbing mountains.

"Well," I said. "It's only a big hill."

"But you did it," she insisted, her face going a little grave, as though she were concerned that I might not appreciate the importance of what Brooke and I had done, "and that's really neat."

"Well, thank you," I said. "I think you are pretty neat."

She gave me a hug and said, "Happy birthday."

▲ ▲ ▲

Marsha said, "You know, I didn't believe you when you said you were going to do it. I never really believed it until we got on the airplane. And once I did believe it, I hated it."

She'd been apprehensive; I'd known that. But I hadn't been sensitive enough to realize how apprehensive she was. It had a lot to do with Brooke, of course. Half of my wife's family was involved in this stunt of mine, instead of the usual 25 percent. But my insensitivity was helped along by a good acting job on her part. I wasn't the only one who hadn't known.

"I thought you were all for it," Brooke said.

"Me, too," Leigh said.

"Then, you should have seen her today," Hadley said.

"Worried?" I said.

"Real worried," Hadley said.

"I wasn't worried," Marsha insisted. "I was just a little nervous."

"We came back from getting your cake," Hadley said, "and when she got your message, she started crying."

"*Hadley,*" Marsha said.

"Well, you did."

"Don't be a snitch. Anyway, I was just relieved."

We ordered our dinners at the Silver Stream and the waitress brought the closest thing she could find to champagne glasses. She didn't seem to mind when I asked her to bring some for Brooke and Hadley, then poured a little for them so they could toast my birthday and, more important, the successful climb. Though we were in a strict Mormon valley, the waitress seemed to understand.

We were having fun but there was something a little disconcerting about the attention. I was used to being embarrassed when people sang happy birthday in a restaurant, making you the unwanted center of attention, so it wasn't that. The disconnect was between the fuss Marsha, Leigh, and Hadley were making over the climb and what I knew—and I suspect Brooke knew—to be the reality. Going up the Grand, if you have never climbed and are considering it, looks like very serious business, something that is both dangerous and physically demanding.

Now that we had done it, and done it with guides, Brooke and I were able to appraise it a little more objectively. We might have gone up in an airplane, but we were not pilots. We had, however, seen real pilots at work.

Still, it was nice then and nice later, with friends back home, to have people admiring something you'd done and carrying on like it was something way out on the edge, even if you knew it wasn't. But even on that first night, tired and light-headed from the intoxicating combination of fatigue and champagne, I was already thinking that I would like more, that this was not a onetime thing. Climbing, it turned out, appealed to me as strongly as I'd thought it would when I first got the notion to climb the Grand, all those years ago. Now that the idea had shape and specificity, it was even more alluring. I knew how a move out on exposed rock looked and felt, and I liked the feeling.

So as I answered questions that night, from my family and Leigh, and later from interested friends, I tried not to make too much of the thing. This was not absolutely false modesty. I thought about that climb every day and it was a wonderful memory. But I wasn't fooled that I had done anything special, and I was sure that this was no one-shot. I wondered if Brooke felt the same and hoped that she did.

"Well," Leigh said, raising his glass as we finished the champagne, "here's to the two of you and your adventure. I'm glad you've got that out of your system."

I smiled and nodded in a noncommittal fashion.

We all drank. Then I blew out the candles on a yellow cake that had white icing, a decoration that looked something like a profile of the Grand, and five candles. One for each decade.

"Best birthday yet," I said. And meant it.

Back to Earth

Mountaineers in print rarely do justice to themselves or the dignity of their subject. —Robin Fedden

There was no climbing when we got home. It was back to work for me and back to school for Brooke, where she continued to work hard, do well, and feel lonely and out of place. But she was determined not to quit.

Marsha visited her frequently. I sent her letters and Gary Larson cartoons that I found especially funny and clipped from the papers. I found an article on Lynn Hill, a rock climber so good that it wasn't sufficient to call her the greatest woman rock climber. Hill had free-climbed the "Nose" of El Cap in Yellowstone in a single day, which was a breakthrough in climbing that compares with the four-minute mile. I found a poster of Lynn Hill and sent it to Brooke to hang on her dormitory wall.

Meanwhile, I was reading everything I could put my hands on about climbing and talking to other magazine writers who either were climbers or knew something about climbing. One of these telephone acquaintances had grown up in Massachusetts. He lived to climb and he told me, during one of our phone sessions, that when he was a student at Amherst, he and some buddies had done a lot of climbing near where Brooke was in school.

"Really," I said. "Where?"

"Best place is called Rose Ledges."

"How far is it from the school?" I said.

"Easy walk," he said. "You should tell your daughter about it."

I did. It was during an especially low time for her. She was trying to show a good face and come on strong, but you could tell.

"You ought to go climbing," I said. "That would take your mind off school for a couple of hours."

"There's no place to go," she said.

"Yes, there is," I said and repeated what my friend had told me.

"I don't have anyone to climb with," she said. "And, anyway, there's no time."

"How about after class?"

"I have to run."

The school had compulsory athletics. Which was good in theory. Sports are good for getting kids out of their rooms and out of their self-absorbed cocoons. But team sports can simply reaffirm, for some kids, their sense that they don't fit in. Brooke swam and ran cross-country and played lacrosse. I don't believe she enjoyed any of them. Her cross-country coach praised her for her dedication and her willingness to train when she was hurt. But that seemed only to emphasize a point Brooke seemed increasingly to be making about herself: that she was a loner and a stoic by temperament. A climber, in other words.

Maybe there were other kids in school who had done some rock climbing, I said. Or who would like to try. Maybe she could put together a club. I was careful to suggest, not insist.

"I don't know," Brooke said. "The school probably wouldn't let us do it."

"Get someone from the school to help you." Brooke was close to a fiery little Welshman who taught chemistry. Dick Gyns was one of those prep school teachers vividly remembered by students long after they have forgotten just about everything else about their prep school years. Happily, Gyns was a passionate outdoorsman.

Brooke spoke to him and he was intrigued by the notion of a rock-climbing club. "Great idea," he said. "Lots more fun than chasing a soccer ball around the bloody pasture." He helped her draft an announcement for the school paper and a petition for the administration. Brooke suspected—and I agreed—that the school would probably resist, for reasons of liability exposure if nothing else.

But private institutions have a way of cutting to the chase. The club was approved and modestly funded. Gyns was named faculty adviser and coach. Some ten kids, including Brooke, joined up. Climbing became her outlet. When she called home, she liked to tell me about the increasingly difficult moves she was making up on Rose Ledges.

I would tell her, when we had these conversations, that I wasn't doing any actual climbing but I'd been reading a lot of books by and about climbers. I was becoming an armchair mountaineer, I said. I hadn't really believed there was such a thing. I could understand someone who read widely and ravenously about, say, the Civil War. But climbing? It seemed to me that if you were that interested in climbing, then you would go out and do it instead of sitting in a room reading about it.

But I was too busy to go as far as I needed to go and take as much time as I needed to take to do some actual climbing. So I read the books, and a lot of what I read was very good. I read *K2, the Savage Mountain*, and *Annapurna*, which were stories of epic climbs on 8,000-meter mountains. Classics, both. The K2 expedition, which included one of the legendary close calls in mountaineering—known in climbing circles as, simply, the belay—ended in failure and death. The Annapurna expedition was the first to reach an 8,000-meter summit. But it also came at a price.

A few of the books—usually those I enjoyed most—were less inclined to the tragic, more to the human sense of awe and delight in the face of nature. I especially liked H. W. Tilman, a wonderful specimen of the eccentric British explorer. There was a touch of Evelyn Waugh in Tilman, who had ridden a bicycle across Africa and reached an altitude of some 28,000 feet on Everest in 1938 while dressed in tweeds. When he was recruiting a crew for an Arctic expedition, 20 years later, he placed the following priceless ad in the *London Times:*

Hands wanted for long voyage in small boat; no pay, no prospects, not much pleasure.

Many of the books I read were old, and often they were out of print. But there were some good contemporary writers. David Roberts, who wrote a number of stories for *Outside* magazine, where I was also a contributor, wrote with precision and a deep feeling for the sport. He was a graduate of Harvard and a member of its mountaineering club. He had made a number of bold climbs in Alaska, including some first ascents. He was that rare thing—someone who could do a difficult, specialized thing and then step back and treat it dispassionately and with the clinical distance of a gifted novelist. I read everything he wrote about climbing and wrote him a fan letter or two.

Roberts was a writer first and a climber second and, among people currently writing about climbing, he was sui generis. Most of the climbing books back then were written by people who were passionate about climbing and workmanlike with their prose. They had experienced things they felt compelled to write about, and the closer those experiences came to disaster and, even, death . . . the stronger the book.

There were, it seemed, a lot of books around about climbs that went bad. There was *Touching the Void,* a climber's account of how he had cut the rope after his partner fell and was pulling them both to certain death. And there was *The Breach*, the title being a description of the mountain wall that was the objective of a climb and the emotional conflict between a climber and his partner. And finally, there was *Nanda Devi*.

This book is an account of one of the more baleful and controversial climbs of the modern era, one that presaged the Everest catastrophe described by Jon Krakauer in *Into Thin Air.* The author of *Nanda Devi*, John Roskelley, was one of the climbers on this 1976 expedition and one of the strongest high-altitude climbers in the world at that time. But the focus of the climb was the 22-year-old daughter of Willi Unsold, whose father had named her after a Himalayan peak he had first seen in 1949. That mountain, which is 25,645 feet high, is called Nanda Devi, which translates to "Goddess of Joy," in Hindi.

Unsold and his daughter were both members of the 1976 expedition. He was one of the most celebrated American climbers of his generation, still famous in mountaineering circles for the high bivouac he survived after summiting Everest in 1963, an ordeal that cost him nine toes but did not stop him from climbing. He was a climber from the old school—more romantic than pragmatic, a free spirit and an extrovert with a playful personality. Unsold, in his fifties, was nearing the end of his career as a high-altitude climber.

Though she did not have her father's experience or technical expertise, Nanda Devi Unsold was, according to people who knew her, an exuberant, bright, and compelling personality. "She was," says Al Read, who knew her, "just an exceptional person. The kind you just like to be around."

The expedition, with its romantic goal of getting this young woman to the top of the mountain she had been named for, foundered on personality conflicts, bad weather, bad judgment, and bad luck. Roskelley made the summit. Before she could make her own attempt, Nanda Devi died in a tent at 24,000 feet. Her father had just stepped outside.

She had been experiencing a hernia—though not suffering from it—and some of her teammates wanted her to go down. She refused and her father, it seems, did not attempt to force her. He let her make up her own mind and she was determined to press on to the summit. She probably died from peritonitis. The condition was not altitude related . . . except that high on the mountain, the necessary medical help was not available.

Devi Unsold's father and two other climbers zipped her into a sleeping bag and dropped her off the mountain, as though it were a burial at sea. They had, Willi Unsold said, "committed her body to the mountain."

His own descent, through a storm, was a terrible ordeal that he barely survived. One wonders if, at some moments, he may not have wanted to.

"Willi had a gray beard and gray hair, flecked with red," one of the other climbers on the descent remembers, "and after we had gotten back to base camp and had a night's sleep, I was shocked when I saw him. His beard and his hair had turned completely white, in less than two days. You read about things like that but you don't really believe they happen. He was devastated."

Less than three years later, Willi Unsold was killed in an avalanche on Mount Rainier.

Nanda Devi was, for the obvious reasons, a book that stayed on my mind.

▲ ▲ ▲

After a while I began looking for climbing stories that were not unrelievedly grim. Climbing was hard and it was dangerous, especially at the extremes. There was no getting around that. But there had to be more to it than sheer, simple masochism. Or exhibitionism, in the case of the book writers.

These books, and these writers, seemed to miss an entire aspect of climbing that made it seductive to me. The climbers I admired through their legends, like Yvon Chouinard or Glen Exum, or limited personal acquaintance, like Alex Lowe, were hardly grim. They were free spirits, full of an exuberant ability to enjoy life. You could be absolutely cold to the idea of climbing and still wish you could borrow some of that. But it was hard to find in the contemporary writing about climbing.

Which is why, I think, I was taken by a little volume called *Blind Corners*. It came in the mail one day and I was intrigued. It could have been that the introduction was written by Sir Edmund Hillary (not "Ed") but for whatever reason, I started reading and did not stop until the last page. The author, Geoff Tabin, was a medical student with a hunger for climbing that he fed by periodically taking off from his studies and signing on with an expedition that needed a medical person. This was an old climbing tradition. Good doctors needed to be just fair climbers to get on expeditions where, if you were strictly a climber, then you needed to be great to have a chance. These days good video artists who are fair climbers are in the same position.

Tabin actually was better than fair as a climber. He was good. Being a medical person, this meant that he got onto some very desirable expeditions. At the time he wrote his book (1993), he was one of the few people in the world who had been to the top of the fabled seven summits. Just a few pages into his book, however, and it was evident to me that Tabin was not merely some trophy bagger and exhibitionist. He loved mountains, loved climbing, loved the camaraderie that develops on an expedition. His enthusiasm was childlike and so infectious that I wrote a review of his book, singing its praises.

It was a couple of months before the review was published and I missed it. So when the phone rang in my office one day and the caller said, "Hi, this is Geoff Tabin," I thought he had the wrong number.

"Yes," I said.

"Is this Mr. Norman?" the caller said.

"Yes."

"Well, this is Geoff Tabin. You reviewed my book."

I suspected that I was talking to someone with a grievance and tried to remember if I had given harsh reviews to any books recently. And wondered who had given the caller my number.

"Mountain climbing," the caller said helpfully.

I was drawing a total blank.

"Introduction by Edmund Hillary."

"Oh, *yes*," I said and began apologizing. I'd written books and I knew how you felt about them and how much it hurt when you realized other people did not, to say the very least, share your feelings.

"I'm sorry," I said, "I'm kind of distracted today . . . working on a deadline . . . wasn't paying attention . . . didn't quite catch your name at first . . ."

"You want me to call back?" he said.

"No, no," I said. "I was just finishing up." This wasn't exactly the truth but I felt guilty for not recognizing the man's name, and also I sensed an opportunity to talk about climbing, which seemed a lot more desirable than whatever it was I'd been doing.

"Well, I just wanted to thank you for the review of my book," he said.

"I should thank you," I said, "for the book."

"You must be a climber," Tabin said.

I was tempted to say yes, and let him draw his own conclusions about how good I was. I might have done that if I hadn't liked his book so much and felt its author deserved straight answers.

"No," I said. "Not really."

"You must have done some climbing."

"Just enough," I said, "to wish I'd started sooner and done a lot more."

I wound up telling him about my summit of the Grand, which was beginning to loom larger and larger in my memory and, at the same time, seem more and more puny when I told the story to anyone who knew about climbing. I felt like someone who has handled the controls of a Cessna 185 for a few minutes talking to an aviator who lands F-14s on a carrier deck.

But Tabin was indulgent, even appreciative, and I decided that it had to be because he felt like he owed me.

"We ought to go climbing together sometime," he said. "You could bring your daughter."

It was the kind of thing people say like, "let's have lunch," though there was something a little baroque about a couple of strangers talking casually about getting together sometime and hanging off the face of a cliff. I said something about how that sounded like a real good idea, feeling certain it would never happen.

"You're not that far from the Gunks," Tabin said. "I've got to be there for a wedding in three weeks, what do you think?"

"If you're serious . . ."

"Absolutely . . ."

▲ ▲ ▲

So I wound up sending Tabin's book to Brooke with a letter telling her that we'd been invited to climb with him and was she interested. She called a couple of days later.

"This is such a cool book," she said.

"I thought you'd like it."

"Does he really want us to go climbing with him?"

"He says so."

"That is so cool."

"So you want to go?" I said.

"For sure," she said. "Don't you?"

"I just wonder if it won't be a little awkward," I said. "I mean, the man has been to the summit of Everest."

"Hey, Dad," Brooke said, "Alex Lowe has been to the summit of Everest, too. And we climbed with him."

"But we paid him."

"I see your point," Brooke said. She thought for a minute, then added, "but he did ask you. He didn't have to do that."

"Right."

"And it's the Gunks, Dad. Remember how Alex Lowe told us some of the best rock climbing in America was in the Gunks."

I'd forgotten. But I remembered now. The Shawangunk Mountains, outside of New Paltz, a couple of hours from New York City, are to the East Coast as Yosemite is to the West.

"How bad can it be?" Brooke said. "And anyway, he doesn't sound like the kind of guy who is going to get all wrapped around the axle if one of us can't make some 5.9 move. He'll see we're just beginners and he'll be cool with it."

"Ummm," I said.

"I think we should go for it."

So I wrote a letter to the school, clearing Brooke's absence for that weekend. I ran a little more than usual, though there wasn't much chance I was going to get myself into iron-man shape in three weeks. I also went to the Mountain Goat, our local climbing and outdoor sports outfitter, and bought a new pair of climbing shoes. When I got home, I put them on and laced them tight and put my feet in a bucket of water until the rough-out leather of the shoes was saturated. I wore the shoes around the house the rest of the day, hoping to mold them to my feet. An old climber's trick that I'd read about somewhere.

The rubber portion of climbing shoes, which wraps the climber's foot, is made of the same stuff that is used on airplane and race-car tires. It was designed to stick on runways and high-banked turns, so it adheres nicely to sheer rock faces. Wearing them inside, I felt like I was glued to the floor. Also, each step produced a squeaking noise that sounded like a cat in distress.

In the middle of the afternoon, one of my wife's friends came by to pick her up for a golf game. Marsha wasn't quite ready, so I got the door. I greeted her friend and asked her in. I led her through the kitchen, walking like I had some kind of crippling condition and squeaking like I needed to be oiled.

She looked at me with real concern in her face, like she might have blundered into the middle of some kind of experimental therapy and should apologize and get the hell out.

"New climbing shoes," I explained. "Just breaking them in."

"Oh," she said. "Of course."

"They're wet now, but when they dry out, they'll fit my feet like a pair of old gloves."

I imagined that Marsha gave the woman a fuller explanation on the way to the golf course. Or, maybe it never came up.

Hanging in the Gunks

The Gunks were the academy of my mountaineering youth. —David Roberts

I met Brooke in front of her dormitory on Friday afternoon. I was early and I'd been there for 15 or 20 minutes, enjoying the languid mood of a campus in the springtime, when she came jogging down the street, carrying a small pack.

"Am I late?" she said.

"No, I'm early. Where have you been?"

"Climbing," she said. "I left early. The other kids and Gyns are still up on the ledges. I did 5.9 today."

"Then you're ready," I said.

She needed to get some things, so she left her pack with me and went inside. The pack was unzipped and I could see that it held her harness and climbing shoes. I wondered if she'd worn them wet around the dormitory to break them in. Probably not, I thought. The other girls would have thought she was strange, and you would do anything in adolescence to avoid that.

Out on the wide green lawn in front of Brooke's dorm, two kids threw a Frisbee and several couples lay on blankets pretending to study. Several kids walked by, moving at the unhurried pace of students who have the entire weekend ahead of them.

Entire lives, too, I thought.

They looked untroubled, almost serene, but of course, they were not. Under the veil of calm, all the usual adolescent storms were brewing. It didn't make any difference how privileged these kids were, they suffered all the common teenage woes. And some—those who were truly out of place here, like my daughter—felt them more acutely.

I'd had my own times like that, when I'd been her age. I'd felt alone and out of it, incapable of doing or saying any of the things it took to be accepted. Solitude had seemed like a very heavy load.

I eased those adolescent burdens in the woods and on the water. Nothing worked for me like fishing or hunting, especially fishing. Instead of television, I had the fishing magazines. Instead of working on cars or playing sports, I went fishing. Later on, when the storms had all passed, I realized they hadn't been so bad, after all, and anyway, I had enjoyed some real good fishing while the other kids were hanging out, impressing each other with their coolness. But nobody could have told me that, or much of anything else, during the bad times.

I wondered what Brooke had to help her through. And what Hadley would have when it was her turn. I knew that Brooke had her work. She was a good student, which could be both good and bad. It took your mind off things when you were deep into the books, but it also increased your sense of isolation.

Did climbing—and her climbing club—do for her what fishing had done for me? No way for me to know. I could ask and she would tell me what she thought I wanted to hear. I hoped that the climbing helped. And that this weekend would turn into a memory she could use when she needed it.

"What are you looking at," Brooke said. She had come through the dorm door without my noticing and was standing next to me.

"Nothing," I said. "You ready?"

"Yes."

"Then, let's get going."

▲ ▲ ▲

The sun set while we were on the interstate so we drove in darkness, which, for some reason, always seems to make talking easier. We didn't talk about Brooke's struggles with the social side of school. She didn't bring it up and I didn't ask. We talked, instead, about her studies. She had an American history course that she liked a lot. They'd been reading about the Civil War so we talked about Gettysburg.

A few months earlier, in the fall when she was going around looking at schools where she thought she might apply, I had driven her down to Washington, D.C., to visit Georgetown. On the way, we listened to a reading on tape of *The Killer Angels*, the masterful novel of Gettysburg by Michael Shaara. We got to Gettysburg after dark and found a motel. In the morning Brooke got up early to run. It was still cross-country season and she was in training.

She went out a road that took her to the McPherson farm, where the first shots of the battle were fired and General Joshua Reynolds, one of the abler Union commanders, was shot out of the saddle and killed. There was a large monument to Reynolds just off the road Brooke took. It was one of scores of monuments in stone and bronze that gave this ground its haunted, sanctified feel.

Brooke was subdued when she got back to the motel.

"It almost feels like you're in church," she said.

We ate breakfast and then we walked to the battlefield. We had the usual tour books and a tape to listen to, and we also had all the images from *The Killer Angels* fresh in our minds. We spent much of the morning in Devil's Den and on Little Round Top, where Joshua Chamberlain's Maine troops had made their desperate bayonet charge and broken the Confederate attack

that could have rolled up the entire Union line if it had succeeded. Chamberlain was one of the central figures in *The
Killer Angels*, a man Shaara plainly found fascinating. He had
survived the war and gone home to run Bowdoin College for
many years. Brooke had told me, when we were talking about
colleges for her, that a lot of her classmates were applying for
Bowdoin. I asked her if the school interested her and she said
no. Emphatically. She'd had enough of small schools in small
towns where all the students knew each other. She wanted a
big university in a big city with the kind of freedom that comes
with anonymity.

After Little Round Top, we walked the Peach Orchard and the
Wheat Field, where the action of the second day ended in bloody,
appalling stalemate. From there we went to Cemetery Ridge and
stood on the little copse, which had been the high-water mark of
the Confederacy, and looked back toward Seminary Ridge and
felt the inevitable chill when we pondered the open ground that
George Pickett and his men had to cross under fire.

That had been a good trip together so we talked about it on
our way to the Gunks, remembering the battlefield tour and
what we had seen. That seemed to be a rule with us. The good
times we'd had gave us something to remember and to talk
about. Families build a fund of memories, I suppose, and live off
the interest.

▲ ▲ ▲

We checked in at a cheap chain motel outside of New Paltz,
New York, and after we'd unpacked we went out to eat. We
drove down the main street of town and settled on a pizza place
where both the customers and the help were college students
from SUNY. We ordered and while we were waiting, I asked
Brooke if she would be interested in going to school here.

"You'd be close to the best rock climbing in the East," I said.
"At least, that's what we've been told."

She shook her head.

"Why not?" I said. "It's a good school."

"I know," she said.

"So?"

"I don't know," she shrugged.

"Too close to home?"

"Sort of . . . but not exactly," she shook her head and thought for a moment. "This just seems kind of *familiar.* Know what I mean?"

"Sure," I said.

It wasn't that this place—or a lot of other places we had talked about and visited—was too close to home. The problem was . . . it was too much like home. She was ready for something different; she wanted to get away in the truest sense. She didn't require a lot of distance, just a lot of difference. It was an old story and I understood because I'd been there, wondering if it was possible to be any farther out of it than in the panhandle of Florida. But like everybody in history, I'd never thought *my* kid would feel this way. As eager as she was to move on out into the world, that was how much I wanted her to stay close.

This trip, I thought, would be going into the memory fund. And there probably wouldn't be a lot like it in the future. This might even be the last one and I could be living off the interest for a long time. It was inevitable, of course, but that didn't make me like it any better.

The pizza came and we talked about other things. Then we went back to our inelegant lodgings and went to bed. It was still fairly early but we didn't know what to expect from Geoff Tabin and the legendary Gunks. We both wanted to be strong in the morning.

▲ ▲ ▲

The drive out to the mountain was unspectacular, even in the early morning light. The road crossed flat farmland, grainfields, and apple orchards, but we could see the long ridge ahead of us, and as we got closer, the cliffs at the top of the ridge became more distinct. They were very white against the green, early spring foliage.

"That must be where we're going," I said.

"I can't believe how big it is."

The cliff did, indeed, seem very long. Maybe as much as a mile long, below a flat plateau that could have been drawn up by the creator for the convenience of rock climbers. Even from a distance, it looked like that cliff would accommodate hundreds of climbers, side by side, all of them taking a different route to the top.

We reached the base of the ridge and began taking a series of hairpins and switchbacks, one of which passed almost directly under the cliff as it soared on up so abruptly that I couldn't see all the way to the top. Brooke and I looked to see if any climbers were already up on the rock. We didn't see any, but it was still very early. I was worried about missing Tabin, so we were among the first cars in the little parking lot on an overlook above the valley. One of the other vehicles was a Volkswagen van that looked a lot like the one that belonged to the climber who had stood under the eaves with us in the rain in Moose, Wyoming. The van was parked next to a vintage Porsche. We were in a Ford pickup and that, somehow, seemed right.

We shouldered our packs, crossed the highway, and took the trail according to the directions Tabin had given me. We were half an hour early when we reached our landmark—a large steel chest where the rangers stored emergency rescue equipment. It was cool and we were wearing canvas shorts and T-shirts. We had fleece pullover jackets—standard climber garb—in our packs and put them on. I had a thermos that had been filled by the waitress at the restaurant where we ate breakfast. We sipped coffee, shivered in the cold, and looked up at the high mute cliffs above us.

The cliffs were not especially tall here. They were also very smooth. I wasn't sure I could handle them. I kept studying them for holds and didn't see many.

Through the trees I could make out a second, much higher set of cliffs. These appeared slightly rougher. I'd been told that the salient characteristic of the Gunks, as far as climbers were concerned, was not the steepness or the height, but the serrations of rock—extruded quartz—that left prominent holds for the climber. For some reason, these were known as buckets in climbing jargon. I liked the sound of that.

I finished my coffee. We spoke to several climbers who went by us on the trail on their way to some starting point for their first climb of the day. Everyone was friendly with the extra measure of bonhomie that comes at the start of a day you have been looking forward to for a long time. The morning is all possibility but the waiting is also over. It is a wonderfully keen and brief moment.

I was feeling it, too, and wanted to get on with the program. I checked my watch. We'd been here almost 45 minutes and Tabin was 15 minutes late. I wondered if he'd forgotten us, run into trouble and tried to call. Maybe I'd gotten the directions wrong and he was waiting somewhere down the trail.

"We'll give it another 15 minutes," I said, "then we'll split up and look for him."

"What if we don't find him?"

"I guess we don't climb," I said. "Unless you want to lead."

Brooke had learned a lot on Rose Ledges and had led a few climbs.

"Would you trust me?"

"Yes," I said, hoping it didn't come to that.

"I'm not sure it would be a good idea," she said.

"We'll see."

I checked my watch and thought about it. We had the guidebook that illustrated and diagramed the established routes.

Maybe we could find some nice 5.3 or 5.4 route and work on our technique. Strange to think of following Brooke up a mountain, counting on her to place protection. And hard to imagine myself agreeing to her going out on lead, counting on her protection and my belay but, in reality, depending on her not to fall. Leaders, the climbing saying goes, must not fall.

I was still working through the dilemma when Geoff Tabin came running up the trail. I'm still not sure where I would have come down if he had not arrived when he did.

"Are you the Normans," he shouted when he was still 50 yards away.

"That's us," I said. "And you don't have to run. We're in no hurry."

He was still panting when he reached us.

"I'm so sorry," he said. "I overslept. The reception went very long."

He was smiling and eager, with a fair and almost innocent face and a wide, disarming smile. He was the sort of person you instantly wanted to like. And I suspect most people eventually did.

"We should probably talk on the trail," he said. "It's a beautiful day and it's going to be crowded on the good climbs. There's one I really want to do. It's my favorite."

"We'll follow you," I said.

So we walked briskly another half mile or so down the trail and then cut up through some trees to the base of the main cliff.

"This," Tabin said, "is High Exposure."

It didn't look like much from where we were standing. The rock wasn't especially steep and there were very good cracks for climbing. But I could see that as the rock got higher, it got steeper and that as you went around to the right, where Tabin said the route would take us, you came out onto a huge buttress. I couldn't see the rest of the route, but Tabin said it was vertical and very exposed. Hence the name.

"It's probably the most famous climb in the Gunks," he said. "One of the most famous anywhere."

"Cool," Brooke said.

We got into our harnesses and tied in. Stashed the packs up snug against the rock. Checked each other's knots. Then Tabin started up the rock. He was not a tall man but he moved with lithe assurance. In a few minutes he had climbed to the first belay position and was calling to Brooke.

She didn't move with Tabin's efficiency or speed, but she had plainly learned a lot and gained a lot of confidence climbing with her new school club on Rose Ledges. I was going to be the rookie, I thought, in this group. Well, I had my camera and if it got to the point where I felt like I was holding them back, I would find a place where I could tie off and shoot them going up the cliff.

We'd see.

Brooke made it to the belay ledge with no problem. She called for me and I started climbing. For a minute or two, I felt like I had never done this before in my life. Then it came back to me, like riding a bicycle, and I was on my way up the rock, concentrating on every hold and trying to make every move positive and sure. You don't want to be tentative, I told myself. Be aggressive.

While I didn't have any trouble making the ledge, there was no doubt about the rankings in our group of three. Brooke had gotten a lot better, climbing with her club. I was still back where I'd been in Wyoming. I wasn't used to the idea but didn't have time to dwell on it just now.

Tabin wanted Brooke, since she was the stronger climber, coming up last and cleaning. We tied in and changed around on the ropes. I belayed Tabin as he moved out on a traverse, toward the corner of the big buttress.

When he got to the corner, he was under a shelf that extended about three feet out from the rock face and blocked his way up. It looked just big enough to be what a climber would call an overhang, and it would take a nifty little move to get around it. Tabin called back to us and said to watch carefully how he did it.

I watched carefully and he made it look so easy that I couldn't learn anything. Then he was gone from view but the rope kept paying out through my belay. Finally, when almost all 160 feet of slack was gone, the rope stopped moving. After a minute or two, I heard Tabin shout, "Off belay." The sound seemed to come from a long way off, very high on the cliff.

Now it was my turn.

▲ ▲ ▲

I made the short traverse from the belay point to the little overhang. That was easy enough. But once I got there, I could not remember the effortless moves Tabin had made to get up and over. I had never imagined that I would make them with his grace, but now it seemed like I would not make them at all. Tabin was too far above me to be any help. I hung on to the rock. My feet, in their new, carefully broken-in shoes, were well positioned on a nice wide ledge, so I could take my time and study.

I did not really want to try the little overhang. I felt no confidence in my ability to make it, not without a guide standing right next to me, telling me where to put each hand and foot, giving me the sequence of each move and a little encouragement as well.

But I didn't want to retreat to the belay ledge, either. Certainly not with Brooke watching. What I thought of as pride—and others would call vanity—would not permit it. I was her dad. Just as leaders cannot fall, dads cannot fail. Childish, macho thinking, perhaps, but that's the way I saw it.

"You remember how he did this thing?" I said to Brooke. She was sitting on the belay ledge, maybe 20 feet away, watching and saying nothing.

"I'm trying to," she said. "Is there a place for your right foot?"

I was moving to the right. If I could get that leg a little higher, then that would give me some leverage to move my torso out from the rock face and then curl it around the overhang. Maybe I could then find a hold for my right hand.

"Let's see what I can find," I said. I looked down when I said it. Then up. I had farther to go to get to the top. If I fell, I wondered, and the belay caught me, could I get back to this place and try again?

Maybe. But Tabin might have to let me down to another ledge and then we would all have to down climb and start over.

If I made a move, I wanted to make a good one. My legs were beginning to tremble with the strain of holding my position. I needed either to go for it or to retreat.

I raised my right foot until my knee was flexed and my calf was almost perpendicular to my thigh and my toes found a little point of rock, just wide enough to support them and my weight. I leaned out—way out—and straightened my leg and threw my right hand up over the shelf. My fingers found a hold, a nice one, the thickness of a hotel Bible. I worked my left foot over to where the right one had been, did the same switch with my left hand to where the right had been. Then brought the right foot up, waist high, until it was around and over the ledge, bringing the rest of my body along.

The entire sequence of moves took a couple of seconds, and everything seemed to be ordained or programmed somehow in the junction between mind and body.

"Way to go, Dad. Great move," Brooke said behind me and made my day.

It would have been routine work for thousands and thousands of climbers, but it was a test of my limits and making that move seemed to free up some innate part of me as I made my way up the huge buttress, finding holds so easily that I felt like

I was flowing over the rock. The inherent drama of High Exposure, the quality that makes it the quintessential Gunks climb, is in this section of the route, when you have cleared the ledge and are out on the massive wall, totally exposed, held on the rock by your fingers and toes, with the slender rope to catch you if you fall. With 200 or 300 feet of air between you and the ground, you feel the same sensations as if you looked over the rail from the top of a 20- or 30-story building, only here you lean out into space instead of backing away from the ledge. Here, the height does not inspire dread—"I'm afraid of heights"—but something like elation. The exposure produces adrenaline and that fuels movement and a kind of sublime confidence as one move flows into the next, like a dance.

I was sweating when I reached the top where Tabin was tied off and holding me on belay. Sweating and trembling, though not with fear, so much, as urgency and elation.

I tied in.

"Off belay," I said. I was panting.

"Belay off," Tabin said. He was smiling broadly and holding up his hand for a high five.

I slapped his hand.

"That was fine work," he said. "Congratulations."

I thanked him. Told him how much I appreciated his willingness to lead a couple of novices when he would certainly have rather been on one of the more challenging routes, with some of his expert friends.

"No," he said. "This is special. Climbs like this one got me started. This is where it all begins."

He took the rope from me so he could belay Brooke and I could move down to another ledge where I could tie off, lean out, and take pictures of her as she came up the big wall.

Once that was done, he took in slack until we heard Brooke's voice, thin but clear, "That's me."

I watched the ledge nervously for what seemed like a long

time. Then her hand and wrist appeared. Her fingers found a hold. Gripped it. Her foot and leg came over the ledge, and suddenly, she was over, straightening up and reaching for the next set of holds. She looked small but strong. Her confidence seemed evident and undeniable, even from this distance. Or maybe that was just what I wanted to see.

"She's a strong climber," Tabin said. So either he'd read my mind or I was right. I felt proud, the way a parent does when someone compliments his kid. And, at the same time, I realized I didn't have much to be proud about. Brooke had made herself this good, with no help from me. That little insight caused me to feel a deeper sense of pride and, also, a kind of wistful sense of being more and more a spectator to my children's lives instead of a participant. There had been a time when the girls skied only with us. Then, given the choice, they preferred to go with friends. The same thing would happen with Brooke and climbing. And, eventually, her life—and Hadley's life—would be separate from mine. It couldn't happen fast enough for them, of course.

Me? I was in no hurry at all.

▲ ▲ ▲

I watched Brooke's progress for a moment, then framed her in the lens of my camera, focused, and took a picture. It occurred to me, in one of those vagrant thoughts, that I'd viewed a lot of my daughters' progress in life through a 35mm lens. Well, I would at least have these memories—and these photographs—which was a big improvement on the mall or family time in Vegas.

I took most of a roll, as Brooke made her way up the wall. She was leaning out from the rock, into naked air, totally exposed in the kind of camera pose that makes your stomach heave if you aren't a climber and gives you a little surge if you are. I could have watched her moving up that rock, her face firm with concentration and her blonde hair shimmering in the morning sunlight . . . I could have watched that all day long, just the way I used to watch her sleep in her crib.

She moved too well for that. She got to the top. Took a high five from Tabin. Smiled at me. Then said, "That was awesome."

High Jinks

We rappelled off the top and retrieved our packs. Then got back on the trail.

"Feel like doing another?" Tabin asked.

Brooke and I both said we did.

"I've got a good one," Tabin said. "We'll do Shockley's Ceiling. You didn't have any trouble with High Ex, so Shockley's won't be a problem."

We said that sounded fine.

"You know about Bill Shockley?" Tabin said. "He's the guy who first climbed the route, so it's named for him."

"I don't know anyone by that name," I said, "but it sounds familiar. Famous guy?"

"Notorious might be more like it."

"Oh?"

"Bill Shockley won a Nobel Prize for his work in solid-state physics, and he was a very good rock climber in his time. But those are not the things he's known for."

I remembered now the context in which I'd heard that name. "William Shockley," I said, "wasn't he the one who used to speak on campus and get people stirred up? Some kind of racial controversy."

"That's our Bill," Tabin said. "He knew physics so he thought that made him an expert in genetics. He had some crackpot theory about race and intelligence. Got him a lot of heat."

"Did you know him?"

"No. He'd done his climbing here before my time. People I knew remembered him. Said he was a really sweet guy and a great climber. Just turned out he was also a little nutty."

"Don't a lot of scientists and doctors and people like that get into climbing?" Brooke said. "I think I read that somewhere."

"Well," Tabin said, "I'm a doctor and I'm into climbing."

"See there," Brooke said.

"And I've thought the same thing. There is a guy at MIT named Henry Kendall who just won the Nobel in physics, and he is a great climber. A guy out at Chicago who will probably win it, who is also a climber. Lots of doctors like to climb. One of the famous Gunks climbers treated John Kennedy for his back problems."

"What's the attraction?" I said. "For doctors, I mean. You don't think of them as thrill seekers. Present company excluded."

"Well, I'm not a thrill seeker, either," Tabin said, then smiled. "Well, maybe just a little. But I think doctors and scientists enjoy climbing because it requires focus and problem solving, but it is also a physical release. After a while, in medicine, you start to feel confined. You want to escape. But you can't get away, entirely, from the cerebral. Climbing is a good mix."

I thought about that for a minute and I liked it. I was no scientist, certainly. Far from it. And among the best explanations I could give people for why I liked climbing was the focus that it required. For the time I had been out on the buttress, climbing High Exposure—and I had no idea how long that had been—I had been concentrating completely on the most essential, elemental things. Where to put my hand. How to shift my weight. How far to lean out. And every one of those questions had been important. The intensive life can, just like pleasure, be seductive.

▲ ▲ ▲

Shockley's was technically more demanding than High Exposure. But not, for some reason, as aesthetically pleasing. Perhaps it is hard to sustain a state of near bliss for very long, I thought, and maybe I should just think myself lucky to have experienced it the way I had that morning, on High Ex. Probably I'd been challenged more by Shockley's. Certainly I felt drained when we came down for lunch.

▲ ▲ ▲

We sat in the sun, at the base of the big cliff, eating sandwiches and watching other climbers as they made their way up the face of the rock. It was impossible not to think of them as ants.

"You know, there is another story about Shockley's," Tabin said. "It's better than the story of how it got its name. When you came up the highway, around the hairpin, you saw where the rock came closest to the road?"

"Right."

"Well, that's Shockley's. It's probably the best climb in all the Gunks if you want an audience. So one day, back in the sixties, a guy named Dick Williams really stopped traffic when he made the climb bare-assed."

"Oh, man," Brooke said, "that's great." She has my weakness for stunts, and I had to agree that a 5.9 naked climb on the most famous rock face in America was inspired.

"Is there more to the story?" I said. There didn't have to be, of course. It would have been fine if some climber had just suddenly decided, one day, for the sheer spontaneous hell of it, to climb Shockley's butt naked. But with that kind of story, you expect context.

"Hey, Dad," Brooke said, "maybe the guy just forgot his clothes."

"Could happen."

"It was better than that," Tabin said. "Have you ever heard of the Vulgarians?"

"Like the Goths and Visigoths?"

"Not far from it. The Vulgarians were climbers. Really great climbers who were also children of the sixties. A lot of the most challenging routes around here were put up by the Vulgarians, and they named them, just like Shockley's and High Ex were named by the people who established those routes. You can almost always tell a route that was put up by one of the Vulgarians by the name."

"Like what?" Brooke said.

"Oh, Drunkard's Delight, Groovy, and Morning After. And then there is one that I'd like to climb this afternoon called Cascading Crystal Kaleidoscope. That ought to give you some idea of what they were into."

The Vulgarians, Tabin said, started as merely an ad hoc collection of climbers who were opposed to an established group called the Appalachian Mountain Club, or the Appies, as they were known to the Vulgarians.

The popularity of climbing was on the rise in the late fifties, though it was still a decidedly fringe sport, considered dangerous and extreme. Members of the Appalachian Mountain Club took it upon themselves to regulate climbing in the Gunks, which was a private landholding. The owners agreed, rather passively, with the scheme, since it seemed like a good way to prevent accidents and avoid notoriety. So the Appies came up with a certification program. Climbers who had not completed this certification were not, in theory, allowed to lead climbs in the Gunks. Well-outfitted Appies patrolled the cliff face, demanding proof of climbers' certification.

"And they ran into a whole new kind of climber," Tabin said.

They were students, mostly from NYU. Bohemians, they might have been called, or Beats in these, the waning days of the fifties. They were smart and exceedingly antiauthoritarian, and in this, they anticipated the seismic cultural shift that was about to occur in America.

"They were bold climbers and free spirits," Tabin said, "and they were not about to let anyone wearing Swiss climbing shorts and funny-looking ranger hats tell them they couldn't climb when and where they wanted to."

The struggle between the Appies and the new climbers was brief and bloodless. The new climbers were better than the Appies and they were defiant, quick to mock their inferiors, and inclined to sabotage. They turned one especially unpleasant Appies' parked car over, and they would pour beer on the Appies patrolling the trail from the rocks above, where they were putting up a difficult new route and carrying a six-pack along for a celebration when they reached the top. The Appies fled the field after a few months of low-intensity conflict. There was no more talk of certification and enforcement. If you wanted to climb the Gunks, then you were on your own. Freedom of the hills.

Nobody is sure when this new breed of climbers began calling themselves Vulgarians. It was never a formal designation and there were certainly no membership rules or credentials. The Vulgarians knew who they were and they recognized one another. It was not a club. It was a tribe.

The Vulgarians, Tabin told us, had their own campsites where they would build bonfires and party hard all night. They had their own hangouts and when they came in, the owners took the tablecloths off the tables. Some of them wore a special hat. It was a thin cotton hat that fit snugly and the Vulgarians called it a Turswiry hat. It was a meaningless term. Someone had read a breathless article about cave explorers who were inevitably described as "terse, wiry leaders." The Gunks climbers liked the phrase and decided to give the name to the hat. *Sports Illustrated* later published an article on Jim McCarthy, one of the great Gunk climbers, and described him wearing "a Turswiry hat." The validation was complete.

There was even a Vulgarian magazine, Tabin went on. It was nothing more than some mimeographed sheets held together with staples. The writing and illustrations were both crude and scatological. The magazine was called the *Vulgarian Digest* or, inevitably, *VD*.

The word got around after a while. Climbing was becoming more popular, and there was eventually a sort of Vulgarian legend that grew up in the community of climbers. It was passed along from one climber to another, and some of the stories no doubt grew larger in the telling. These were new times. Kerouac, who had actually done some climbing, was giving way to the spirit of Ken Kesey and the psychedelic bus. Outrageousness was an art form and it seemed almost logical that if you aspired to climb high, then you would also get high. The Vulgarians were the Merry Pranksters of their own subculture.

"One night at a campsite out West somewhere," Tabin said, "there were a bunch of climbers sitting around talking and doing what people did in those days. One of the Gunks climbers was there—hitching from mountain to mountain, probably—and he told some of the Vulgarian stories. Later on, this kid came up to him and said he wanted to be a Vulgarian and who did he have to talk to about joining up. The Gunks climber told the kid, 'Listen, there's no membership. If you think you're a Vulgarian, you probably are. And if someone who is a Vulgarian thinks you are, then you *definitely* are.'"

The Vulgarians, like the era that spawned them, lost coherence and finally just went away, becoming lost in the mists of time and nostalgia. People grew up, got married, started families, lost themselves in their careers or in serial misfortunes. In the memory of some people, those remain the best of times.

"That climb Dick Williams made nude," Tabin said, "was the ultimate Vulgarian statement. A photographer went with him, taking pictures. Later on, when Dick opened a climbing business in town, called Rock and Snow, somebody put up a poster showing almost all of the owner, making his most famous climb. That poster was there for years."

"What happened to it?" Brooke said.

"I guess people got tired of looking at it. It was an old story. I heard Williams did the climb again, a couple of years ago, on the twentieth anniversary of the first climb. But it wasn't the same."

"Not outrageous anymore," Brooke said.

"No. Just sort of cute," Tabin said. "Hard to imagine what would be outrageous these days."

▲ ▲ ▲

We climbed the route called Cascading Crystal Kaleidoscope—or CCK—that afternoon. It was more difficult than anything we'd done that morning, and I took a hard fall. I went only a few feet before Tabin caught me on the belay, but I hit the rock wall hard enough that I lost my watch, an old and battered Tag Heur that probably wasn't worth much to anyone except me. I was more embarrassed by the fall than anything else.

"What happened?" Brooke said. She'd been watching from a ledge below, waiting to follow me and clean the protection.

"I got squeezed in an open book," I said. "Bad habit of mine."

"Are you all right?"

"Never better." Which was true. I felt oddly relieved, and even exhilarated to have fallen.

I finished the climb and took pictures from the belay position as Brooke came up. She did fine, especially on an overhang that had given me trouble and which she handled nimbly.

It was mid-afternoon and we were all at the top. Tabin seemed a little restless and I imagined that he probably had friends somewhere on the mountain and that he would rather have been climbing with them, on routes that were a lot more difficult than anything Brooke and I could do. I told him that I'd had enough for the day and he seemed relieved, like a scratch golfer who is finally free of an 18 handicapper.

Brooke and I thanked Tabin again. Sincerely. He wasn't our guide, exactly, though he had certainly been guiding us all day. We'd never have made those climbs ourselves, without some sort of guide. But Geoff Tabin was doing a surgical residency at Mass General. He was not a professional guide or a full-time climber. Not some itinerant rock jock who lived to climb. We'd spent the day like friends—casual friends, bound by a single interest—and I'd liked that. Brooke liked it, too. And we both liked Tabin.

"Let's stay in touch," I said.

"For sure," he said.

It had been another good day of climbing, and just then the future looked promising for more days like this. Which was fine with me; I felt like I couldn't get enough.

All Climbed Out

As I lay, and rested, and looked out, I determined that this should be my last great ascent. . . . The mountains, as I looked at them now in turn, looked to me—just mountains.
— Geoffrey Winthrop Young

I went back to the Gunks several times over the next few months, always with Brooke. I got better but I never caught up to her, and that bothered me less and less. She could lead and keep pushing up in her life, as she seemed determined to do; I couldn't have stopped her if I'd wanted to. She was making her college and her career plans, mapping out a life where she was no longer anyone's baby.

So the climbing became what we had together. Marsha would drive over to see her, almost every week, and they would go out to dinner and talk for two or three hours. They were developing the kind of intimacy that mothers and grown daughters have when they are lucky. It didn't include me and I didn't mind. Brooke and I had the climbing, which had begun by accident and turned into something neither of us could have imagined. It wasn't our only bond—wouldn't have worked if it had been—but it was how we spent time together and I couldn't think of a better way, though, in truth, I never tried anything else. Maybe the mall would have worked, but I don't think so.

I began to think of other places where Brooke and I would

go to climb—Yosemite, Joshua Tree, the Tetons, again. I also dreamed of the big mountains we would attempt. I assumed we would simply go on climbing together until I got too old to do it any longer, and that seemed years away.

Even though I was still a novice, I had begun to take an off-hand attitude toward the dangers of climbing—to assume, in short, that accidents happened, but they happened to other people. I was, if not good enough, then certainly careful enough that I would never fall. I also assumed this about Brooke. Then we climbed one day with a man who had known Lynn Hill when she was climbing in the Gunks, and he told us about the serious fall she had taken at a place called, eerily, the Styx Wall in Buoux, France.

"She didn't realize that she hadn't tied in," the man told us. "She'd run the rope through her harness but hadn't tied her figure eight. It was just loose ends, hidden under the tail of her sweatshirt."

Hill had finished a long pitch on a difficult route, unaware that she was climbing unprotected, that she might as well have left the rope in her pack. She leaned back, after a hard move, and took her hands off the rock to rest and let the rope take her weight. The point of the rope slid through her harness and she fell, 40 feet.

"She was hurt pretty bad," the man said, "but it could have been a lot worse than that. She was climbing again in a few months. But it goes to show you what can happen."

Yes, Brooke and I soberly agreed, it did that.

Still, we kept going back to the Gunks that summer, and our climbs went off with nothing more serious than some short falls that did not even knock my watch from my wrist. But as much as I enjoyed the warm summer days of rock climbing, in idle moments I would imagine myself much higher, on the cold and forbidding summit of some very high mountain. It became something close to an obsession with me, and I began simply to assume it would happen and that Brooke and I would do it together. I couldn't have imagined it any other way.

▲ ▲ ▲

Brooke went back to school in September. It was her senior year and she had done well. I wanted to give her something special for graduation and hit on the idea of a climb. I even managed to convince myself that my impulse was entirely generous, that there was nothing she would like more than to climb some big mountain with me.

The mountain I had in mind was Denali, the Alaskan mountain that was formerly known as McKinley and, in some circles, still is. It is the highest point on the North American continent, 19,700 feet at some 63 degrees north latitude, making it one of the coldest of the world's major peaks.

I knew that much before I began my research and I learned, fairly quickly, that McKinley was first climbed in 1910 (an earlier claim turned out to be fraudulent and one of the darker chapters of climbing's shady side) and that during the summer, it was climbed by a number of routes. Some of these routes could be handled by novices if they were competent on snow and ice, trained in the use of an ice ax and crampons, able to perform a self-arrest, deal with crevasses, and carry their gear behind them on a towed sled. These were all things that Brooke and I would have to learn, but I told myself it wouldn't be difficult. The White Mountains of New Hampshire were close by, and in the winter they are an excellent place for cold-weather alpine instruction. I knew the head of the Eastern Mountain Sports climbing school from a magazine story I had written years before. Once I had lined up a McKinley expedition that Brooke and I could join and afford, I felt sure I could call Joe Lentini in North Conway and arrange for a few days with him. The best time would be while Brooke was home for Christmas vacation.

After Brooke left for school, I began calling and faxing people, asking for information on McKinley and guide services. I spoke to Al Read of Exum, who remembered me and said yes, his company put expeditions up on McKinley. I asked him if Alex Lowe led any of those climbs and he said no. But he knew guides he was sure Brooke and I would get along with. He sent me his material, which I added to my Exum file. It brought back good memories of the climbing school and the Grand to look over the old correspondence and the certificates Brooke and I had been given for finishing the school and making the summit. I began to look forward to McKinley the same way I had anticipated so eagerly going up the Grand.

I needed to come up with a deposit around Christmas. I managed to get the money and put it aside and thought it would make a good Christmas present for Brooke—an envelope under the tree containing a picture of Denali, white and formidable, with the dates of our expedition written on it in wax pencil and a note explaining that it was a Christmas present as well as a graduation present in advance.

▲ ▲ ▲

Brooke called home one night, during this time, and said that the coach of her rock climbing club, Dick Gyns, was putting together a group of students for a trip to Alaska in the summer and he wanted to include her. She was thrilled. In fact, I'd seldom heard her sound so excited.

I told her that was great and asked her how long she would be gone.

"All summer," she said breathlessly. "We leave a week after graduation and get home at the end of August. The trouble is, it's pretty expensive."

"Well, it is Alaska and you may not get another chance," I said. "Think of it as a graduation present."

▲ ▲ ▲

I was disappointed but not surprised. While I could be obtuse about these things, even I could see the signs. And I had Marsha to explain the facts of life.

"We aren't as important to them as we used to be," she said, "and that's normal. It's all about their peers now."

This was true, of course, for both of us. But she was still close to the girls in a way I could never be. They talked to her when they were troubled, and she was sympathetic and understanding and she had wise things to say. It would never have occurred to them to come to me for intimate advice and conversation. They thought of me, I suppose, in another way. We weren't estranged; they'd merely outgrown me.

I considered going to McKinley without Brooke. I would be part of a team of strangers, with a couple of guides leading us. Based on our experience on the Grand, I thought, my chances of making the summit might even improve if I went without Brooke.

But I decided against it. I told myself it was the money.

▲ ▲ ▲

That spring Hadley used all the money she had saved from baby-sitting to buy a yellow Labrador puppy. The man who sold her the puppy was a professional trainer, and his dog had won field trials. He taught Hadley his techniques and tricks, which she used that summer to train the dog. She had named the dog Tickle My Fancy and called it by the name of Tick.

She went through the training routines in the backyard, giving the dog voice and hand commands and throwing a retrieving dummy. I kept her company and watched and sometimes tossed the dummy as she turned an undisciplined pup into a nearly finished retriever. Marsha and Hadley and I took Tick for a couple of canoe rides on a nearby river and went for long walks on the logging roads that cut through the nearby hills.

It was a good summer and I put climbing behind me, more or less. I even stopped reading about it.

Brooke returned from Alaska and departed almost immediately for Spain. She would be spending the year at the University of Barcelona, learning Spanish and catching her breath, academically, before she came back to the states and enrolled at the University of Chicago. She had come up with that plan on her own, more or less, and she was excited about her new life. Everything that excited her, it seemed, took her a little farther away.

I was in New York on business the day she left the country. She took an Amtrak train from Albany and I met her at Penn Station. The train was late and we took a cab to Kennedy and got there with no time to spare.

"You'll call your mother when your plane lands, right? She'll be worried." For some reason I had to pin it on Marsha. I don't know why I couldn't say *I* would be worried.

"It will be late," she said.

"Doesn't matter. Just call."

She nodded.

"And listen," I said. "I want you to have a great year."

"I will."

"Don't miss anything. Do it all."

She nodded again.

"The only rule is—you have to learn to speak Spanish. You can marry a bullfighter, if you want, but you have to learn to speak Spanish."

She smiled and I felt what all fathers since the beginning of time have felt. A daughter's smile could stop wars. Probably has.

The cab pulled up at Air France departures and we got out. Some kind of terrorist alert was in force so I could not go inside the terminal with her. We hugged and I watched her through the doors, carrying a walkman and her backpack from Alaska.

It seemed like a small container for all her goods. She would be gone for a year.

"Love you, Dad."

"Love you, too. Don't forget to call."

▲ ▲ ▲

I waited around a while on the curb to make sure she didn't reappear, having missed her plane after all. After 30 or 40 minutes it seemed safe to leave, so I caught an airport bus to the subway stop and rode the A train back into Manhattan and Penn Station, where I got on an Amtrak train for home.

The track followed the Hudson River valley north with the sun setting over the mountains and turning the surface of the river the color of a ripe orange. I watched the river and when we were approaching Poughkeepsie, I looked out to the west at the long flattop mountain, now dark against the evening sky. The Gunks, where Brooke and I had climbed together. Where she had climbed, literally and metaphorically, right past me on her own way to the top.

It was a good memory, and I suspected that might be all that it was. That part of the package, it seemed, was complete. Nothing left to do but put a ribbon on it and stick it under the tree.

Big Plans

Cut out the photos and pin them to the wall,
Cut out the map and follow the details of it all,
Follow the progress of this mountain mission,
Day by day let it inspire our lowly condition.
— W. H. Auden and Christopher Isherwood,
The Ascent of F6

I did manage to get to McKinley eventually, but not to climb. Hadley and I went to Alaska while Brooke was still in Spain, finishing her studies. The two of us spent several days flying around the country with a woman named Lori Egge, a former bush pilot who was starting a business she called Sky Trekking Alaska. In addition to being a very competent pilot, Lori had a wonderfully extroverted personality. In her years of flying around the state as a fish spotter and bush pilot, she had made friends with dozens of lodge owners and operators of bed-and-breakfasts. Her plan was to fly clients around the state, according to an itinerary they had agreed on, seeing the sights and staying in comfortable lodging. I was writing a magazine article about Lori and her business.

Lori made an effort with Hadley, who could be shy, and after a few hours, they became friends. Hadley still had the sharp eyes and spotted animals from the air and pointed them out to Lori and me, long before we saw them. Lori was impressed.

When we were not in the air, flying over vast, uninhabited stretches of Alaska, we trekked across glaciers, kayaked among the seals and sea otters, and fly-fished for salmon as they were coming up the rivers to spawn. We spent one especially memorable day sharing a sandbar with four feeding grizzly bears. They were 200 or 300 yards upstream and, more important, upwind from us and no real threat. Still, it was hard to pay attention to your casting or the drift of your fly, especially when one of the bears charged the river after a fish, throwing up a spray of silver water like something had exploded, then emerging with a salmon, still flopping, in its jaws.

"Awesome," Hadley said, after one especially impressive charge. "Go for it."

Later, we were fishing in a pool where the bank was grown up thick with willows, and we heard a chuffing sound and then something breaking branches. It had to be a bear and in those close quarters, it was possible that we could startle the grizzly and provoke a charge.

"Let's get out of here," I said.

"Sounds good to me," Hadley said.

We walked down the bank to a little point of rock where Lori had beached the floatplane and was sitting on the pontoon, waiting and enjoying the sun. Just before we reached the plane, Hadley turned around for some reason. The bear chose that moment to stand up on its hind legs, in order to get up above the willows for a look. It was, Hadley guessed, 30 steps away. They looked at each other across one of those intervals of time that is somehow astonishingly brief and impossibly long. Then, when its curiosity had been satisfied, the bear dropped back down into the grass.

"Wow," Hadley said, "did you see that?"

I hadn't. And when she told me, I wished I had.

"I can't believe it," Hadley said. "I mean, I really can't believe it."

So, it was a fine trip. Hadley and I still talk about it, and usually when we do, the conversation begins with the words, "Remember that bear . . ."

We saw Denali from the air, one afternoon, a long way off, but I didn't feel any special longing to be there. I found myself thinking, in fact, that this might be as close to the big mountain of my dreams as I would ever get and that I could easily live with that.

▲ ▲ ▲

Hadley was outgrowing me, the same way Brooke had. She was more interested in spending time with her peers—including boyfriends, which took some getting used to. My fling with climbing seemed to be over. Marsha and I began to feel, only slightly prematurely, like empty nesters. We took a second honeymoon—to Venice. I missed the old days, I suppose, but the new days weren't bad.

▲ ▲ ▲

I might not have ever gotten back into climbing except, paradoxically, for the publication of Jon Krakauer's book *Into Thin Air*.

This seems, of course, at least slightly irrational. In addition to being a wonderful, gripping book, Krakauer's account of the 1996 Everest calamity should be a cautionary tale for the novice climber. Amateurs who think they are capable of handling big, dangerous mountains stand to be disabused in the cruelest way. Sandy Pittman, the woman Alex Lowe had told me he would be guiding up Everest, was nearly killed on Everest, and Krakauer's account made her out to be the most unappealing kind of dilettante who just about deserved what she got. Two other novice climbers, members of Krakauer's team, did die, and another was hideously disfigured as a result of severe frostbite but very lucky to survive, thanks to an extraordinary, high-altitude helicopter rescue. Three professional guides also perished.

For weeks after the book was published, people I knew talked about it and argued about who, if anyone, was responsible for the catastrophe and about the prudence of climbing big mountains if you were not highly trained or, for that matter, climbing them at all. In these conversations, some people blamed the guides and some blamed the clients. Some seemed to think it was simply bad timing. The climbers were on the summit when a storm came in and perished on the descent. If the weather had just held for a few more hours . . .

I took part in these discussions and found them as interesting as anyone else. In the postmortems, it always seemed to me like the disaster resulted from an accumulation of small, almost trivial errors, no one of which was especially significant. It was the weight of a number of mistakes that finally crushed the unfortunate climbers. I held to this opinion for a couple of years. Until I got to Aconcagua.

But in all these discussions of Krakauer's book, one thing never seemed to come up—at least not among the people I knew and talked with. That is . . . what a marvelous thing it would have been for those people if things had not gone so terribly wrong and they had made the summit, survived the descent, and come home to tell the tale and live with that climb in their memories for the rest of their lives. My mind kept detouring around the images of those desperate climbers, lost in a night blizzard at 27,000 feet, and imagining them, instead, as they cleared the last difficult piece, the Hillary Step, some 200 feet below the summit and they knew, just knew for sure, that they had it in the bag.

It wasn't perversity on my part—I don't think so, anyway—but simple reflex. Something I couldn't help and had no control over. When I thought about the Krakauer book, which was often, I did not wish to be on that climb; but I wanted badly to climb again.

I decided to look, again, for an opportunity to do one big

climb. And to keep the search to myself. If I went by myself, that would be fine.

▲ ▲ ▲

When she was about to start her junior year at Chicago, Brooke told me that she was ahead of schedule for graduation.

"How so?" I said.

She explained that she had picked up some college credits in her last year of prep school and then tested out of the university's language requirement.

"See," she said, "that year in Spain wasn't just about bull-fights and fiestas."

"Well, I'm sorry to hear that," I said. "But does it mean you are going to graduate early?"

"Maybe," she said. "Or I could take some graduate courses. And, I could take a quarter off and work on my thesis or something."

I said something about how it was nice to have options like that and forgot about it. Then it occurred to me that Denali wasn't the only big mountain in the world and that we did not necessarily have to make our big climb in the summer when, for some reason, I always seemed to be busy and she was always working some job to help pay for school. Maybe she could take time off in the winter, now that she was ahead of schedule, and we could climb somewhere else.

I called Al Read of Exum and asked his advice.

"Well," he said, "there is Aconcagua."

I knew about the mountain from my reading. Like Denali, it was one of the seven summits. It was almost 23,000 feet but novices could climb it. And since it was in the Southern Hemisphere, January and February would be the time. And while the travel arrangements would not be as simple as they would for a Denali climb, it would be easier than going to, say, the Himalaya. Aconcagua sits entirely in Argentina, on the western border of the country.

"Most people fly to Santiago, Chile," Read explained. "But you could go in through Mendoza."

"Do you put together expeditions?" I asked.

"Not through Exum," Read said. "But one of our guides usually does a trip to Aconcagua in the winter and takes clients. If he's going this year, you might be able to get on with him."

I asked Read, as diplomatically as I could, if he thought this guide would be right for Brooke and me. I even heard myself using the phrase "personality fit."

"Absolutely," Read said. "He's the same guy I had in mind back when you were talking about Denali. His name is Jim Williams."

▲ ▲ ▲

I could not call Williams, Read explained, because at the moment he was in Nepal.

"He's in Wyoming during the summer," Read said, "and after that, you have to find him. He's got his own business and a secretary in Jackson. Talk to her and she'll tell you how to get in touch with Jim by e-mail."

I called the number in Jackson and spoke to Williams' secretary, who told me, yes, he was leading an Aconcagua expedition early in February and there were still some openings. Did I care to book?

Well, I said, I might. But I'd like to talk to Williams first, if not in person then perhaps by e-mail.

Sure, she said, and gave me an e-mail address. She also said she would put some literature in the mail.

I sent an e-mail to Williams at the address she had given me. I told him who Brooke and I were and what our experience was and said that we might like to join his Aconcagua expedition if he would have us.

He got back to me, a couple of days later, saying that he thought Brooke and I would fit in fine with the group he was putting together. If we wanted to go, we should read over the literature his assistant would be sending and he would talk to us when he got back to the states, sometime around Christmas.

About that time, I got the package from his assistant with forms to be filled out by each client's doctor, releases, contracts, equipment checklists, advice on getting in shape, a map and history of Aconcagua, and a fee schedule along with information about flights to Santiago.

I looked it over with the feeling that, suddenly, things were moving awfully fast.

I called Al Read back and apologized first for bothering him. It seemed like I had used one climb, up the Grand, as a platform to ask him an awful lot of questions.

"Not at all," Read said.

I explained that I was inclined to sign up with Jim Williams and wondered if there was any reason I shouldn't.

"None," Read said firmly.

"That good?"

"The best," Read said. "Professional, mature, experienced. Great climber. All of that. Plus, he has a very outgoing personality and a real gift for leadership. He's great for telling stories and keeping everyone going. I can't recommend him enough."

Which was certainly good enough for me.

"Then, I guess that settles it," I said. "Looks like we'll be going up Aconcagua with Jim Williams."

"That's great," Read said. "Good luck."

I'd made the call from my office, where I was sitting alone. It was late in the afternoon and I had the material Jim Williams' assistant had sent spread out on my desk in front of me along with some of my old climbing files, including the stuff I had put together on Denali and the first brochures I'd brought home from Exum. I started a new file of Aconcagua material, wrote a check to cover the deposit Williams needed, made a note to call about airlines reservations in the morning, then ran off copies of all the things I would need to send to Brooke in Chicago. Finally, I picked up the phone and called her.

"Listen," I said, "if I could put together an Aconcagua trip this February, would you be willing to take off winter quarter?"

"Absolutely," she said, "I'm there."

"Well," I said, "you'd better speak to the dean about a leave of absence. And don't forget to ask if you're still covered by the university's health insurance."

"I'm all over it," she said.

"Good. I'll send you a package."

Last Reservations

Climbing is an exploration of yourself and the conse-
quent deep relationships with your partners. At its most
fundamental level, it's not about conquering a particular
mountain or achieving a specific goal . . . climbing is a
journey with lots of wonderful experiences.

—Alex Lowe

A couple of weeks before Christmas, I was at my desk.
Working, I suppose, though I'd been increasingly distracted by the climb and all the preparations. The phone rang
and I answered automatically.

"Hello."

"Hello," a voice answered with lots of energy and familiarity, like someone you knew and hadn't spoken to in a long time,
"this is Jim Williams."

"Oh," I said. "Hello. When did you get back?"

"Last night," he said, "I thought I'd better give you a call
and see what we need to go over."

I looked at my watch. It was barely nine in the morning in
Wyoming.

"Well, I appreciate your calling."

"Not a problem," he said. It was the first time I'd ever heard
him use that phrase—but certainly not the last. It was, in some
way, Jim Williams' mantra. In his view, virtually nothing was a
problem. Anything that *looked* like a problem could either be

fixed through his ingenuity or overcome through the sheer force of his considerable will.

We talked for an hour or more and he answered my questions in detail and with patience. I had a lot of questions. I wanted to know about many of the items on the equipment checklist. He explained, for instance, what Dachstein wool mittens were and why we needed them as well as climbing gloves. And why we needed both a parka and a down-filled jacket. Why a foam pad was better than an inflatable Thermorest. And so forth.

I made notes on the checklist.

"Now," he said, "I understand you want to do the Polish glacier."

"Yes," I said. This made the last 3,000 feet, or so, a technical climb, requiring ropes, crampons, and ice axes. Otherwise, it was what climbers—and especially, non-climbers who had some knowledge—called a walk-up.

"Well," Williams said, "I think you need to be clear, before we get started, on what that means."

"Okay."

"You need to know," Williams said, "and I need to know what is more important to you. Is it more important for you to make the summit or is it more important for you to do the Polish?"

"I see."

"Now, you've never been on a mountain this big before," he went on, "so you don't really know how you're going to handle the altitude. There isn't any way to know. You could fold before you ever get close to the Polish."

"I understand," I said. It seemed a little odd to be talked to this firmly by someone I had, in effect, just hired. But Williams wasn't strutting and marking territory; I could sense this even over the phone. He was simply getting things out in the open before we got started and were halfway up the mountain, where discussing them for the first time could result in things worse than hurt feelings.

And anyway, I thought, I wanted him to be more than just our guide; I was counting on him to be a leader. There was more at stake than merely getting me up a mountain. My little girl was involved.

"Personally," he went on, "I think if it is the first time you are on a big mountain, like Aconcagua, how you get to the top is going to seem a lot less important than just getting there. You are going to be real unhappy if it turns out you could have summited but didn't because you were determined to do the Polish."

"All right," I said.

"Go ahead and bring what you'll need for the Polish—the extra climbing tool and your helmet, your harness and a couple of locking caribiners—if you are convinced you want to try it," Williams said, a little less sternly now. "We won't know till we get there if it can even be climbed. Some years, there is too much snow and some years there is not enough snow. You just never know. If I decide it doesn't look right, or if you change your mind after the approach, we can always leave that stuff behind at base camp and go up the *Ruta Normal*. And, who knows? The Polish may be in great shape, you and your daughter may not have any trouble with the altitude, and we might just knock it off."

"Let's hope," I said.

"As long as we're clear and we understand each other."

"Absolutely."

▲ ▲ ▲

I called Brooke after Williams and I finished talking.

"Well," I said, "I talked to our guide."

"And?"

"I believe we are in good hands."

▲ ▲ ▲

Brooke came home from Chicago in December. It was Hadley's last year of living at home, and perhaps for that reason or maybe because of what Brooke and I were about to do, it was an unusually poignant and festive Christmas. We did the things we had always done—cutting down the tree, stringing popcorn and cranberries, making gingerbread houses and fruit-cakes—and it all seemed very nostalgic.

On New Year's, my friend Chris Buckley and his wife Lucy came up with their two children. Chris and I had known each other since before I was married. The Buckley kids called me Uncle Jeff, which flattered me. My kids thought Chris was hip and cool and sophisticated and generally one of the funniest people on earth. He wrote best-selling books and was on television, so he was a celebrity, which also counted. Marsha had become close with Lucy over the years and so, for that matter, had I. I told Chris she was the best thing that ever happened to him and for once, that old formulation was correct. We were a lot of people in a little house but we always had a good time. New Year's was something we all looked forward to for the rest of the year.

And, like Christmas, this year's celebration seemed especially sweet. It may have been something I had manufactured in my own mind, but I felt it keenly. My girls were grown and virtually gone. I already missed them.

Long after midnight on New Year's Eve, all of us—except the Buckley children, who were sleeping—went out into the woods beyond my house. The ground was covered with snow and the temperature was in the teens. The air was utterly still and the sky was clear and full of stars. We were drinking champagne from the bottle, laughing at everything and even singing. We did it every year. It felt foolish and wonderfully so.

I had one arm around Marsha's waist, the other around

Chris's shoulder, and I looked up at the sky, my eyes blurring with the cold, and I stared at the stars and the dark profile of the low mountain a mile or so from my house and felt all the predictable sentiments. These were my friends and family. What in God's name was I doing going off to climb some ridiculous mountain in Argentina? And what kind of madness was it to be taking my daughter along?

But I kept those thoughts to myself and in the morning, I was fine.

▲ ▲ ▲

We were due to depart for Santiago on the last day of January—Super Bowl Sunday, as it turned out, which meant that Marsha and I would not be hosting our annual fried chicken, black-eyed peas, cornbread, and pecan pie football party. Our Yankee friends were crushed. It also meant that Brooke and I had to get a lot done in a little bit of time. We repeatedly inventoried our gear and ordered the things we needed, which began to seem like more than we could carry across the street, much less up a mountain. We visited our doctor for physicals and to get prescriptions for antibiotics and a drug called Diamox that can help climbers get rid of fluid buildup that sometimes occurs at altitude. Our doctor, who had been seeing Brooke since she was an infant, was intrigued by our project. His clinic is always busy but he spent 15 or 20 minutes talking to us and earnestly wished us good luck when we left. I took out onetime evacuation insurance policies in case we got sick or injured while we were out of the country and made sure our memberships in the American Alpine Club were current so we would have rescue insurance if we needed help getting off the mountain. We spent three days in the White Mountains of New Hampshire, where Joe Lentini of EMS worked with us on our snow and ice technique. We climbed frozen waterfalls, practiced self-arrest, and did a lot of walking in crampons.

"I'd say you're good for the Polish," Joe said when we were leaving. Then he added one piece of advice, which he aimed at me, "Remember, it is not a race to see who gets to camp first. Make sure you have something left for the summit."

I thanked him and said I would remember.

All this activity was good for keeping doubts at bay and I had plenty of those. They were most active at night when I was otherwise idle.

The mildest of my worries was, simply, that I wouldn't make it to the summit. I had been working out hard, running the hills and lifting weights, for months, ever since I first started making arrangements to climb Aconcagua. But I had never been close to that kind of altitude. I had considered a warm-up climb on one of the high Mexican volcanoes that can be climbed easily on paths that run all the way to the summit. But I didn't have the time or the money. Also, I was—to put it charitably—getting a little old for this sort of thing. I was more than 10 years older than my guide. Most people who climb are in their twenties and thirties, but I had neglected to start then and had been making up for lost time. On a trip to New York, just before Christmas, I had been introduced to a man who was a climber and had done several of the seven summits. "But not Everest," he said, smiling. "Yet."

I asked him if he'd been to Aconcagua.

"Twice," he said. "The first time, I couldn't make it. I went back for another try and almost didn't make it that time. Summit day was, hands down, the hardest thing I have ever done. Never been so tired. Before or since."

The man was 20 years younger than I and he looked like he was in great shape.

Then, a few days before our departure, I was in the Mountain Goat, the local outfitter, for some last small item. I was talking to the owner. We'd known each other for years.

"You know, we have another customer who just came back

from Aconcagua. Good climber. Done a lot in Alaska." He gave me a name, but it didn't mean anything to me.

"Really," I said, "maybe I ought to give him a call. Get some tips."

"You might not like what you hear."

"Oh?"

"He didn't make it. Got about halfway up on summit day and just ran out of gas. He told me he just couldn't believe it was so hard."

"Altitude?" I said, like an old hand.

"I guess."

"That's tough."

"Yeah, well . . . good luck. You'll make it."

▲ ▲ ▲

Not making it, though, was the least of my worries. You can live with disappointment and, in fact, you get better at it as you get older. More practice, I suppose. Worse things could happen to you on Aconcagua than wimping out. You could fall, though that wasn't likely in our case, unless we did the Polish and even then, it was a low-order risk. Still, you could get frostbite and lose fingers or toes. This happened, according to my reading, almost routinely among climbers who were badly equipped or found themselves trapped in storms. Frostbite was definitely bad, but it got worse than that. Climbers died on Aconcagua from hypothermia when, for instance, they became lost and were forced to spend nights without shelter in high winds and subzero temperatures. They also died from pulmonary edema, which is a buildup of fluid in the lungs and from cerebral edema, a similar excess of fluids in the brain. Both these conditions strike climbers at altitude and there is no way of knowing who will be affected. It is also easy to mistake symptoms for normal discomforts of altitude. After the Krakauer book, even non-climbers were aware of all the fatal possibilities in high-altitude climbing. Still, sixteen climbers had died on Aconcagua the year before our climb.

I didn't worry so much for myself; even novice climbers have an ability to simultaneously embrace and deny risk. You do the thing, in part, because it is dangerous, but you are sure you will never get hurt. Certainly not killed.

Still, I worried about Brooke. Not that I thought she was any more likely to get hurt than I was. She was, if anything, less likely. Younger, fitter, temperamentally more careful . . .

No, I worried because she was my daughter and worrying is one of the things parents do best.

Finally, I worried about Marsha because I knew she worried about us. She'd never said anything about it. Certainly never tried to talk me out of going; her mantra in life was *go for it* and I had heard her speak those words a million times and counting. That was the way she did things— everything from horseback riding (which was how she had ruined a knee) to cooking and decorating—and she was too proud to be inconsistent. She believed everyone should live that way, especially if they were family. Even if she didn't like the choices. But I knew and it bothered me. I can't imagine being married to someone for 20 years without developing at least some habits of consideration. It seemed inconsiderate to make her worry for the sake of a stunt.

▲ ▲ ▲

All this ambivalence might have become unbearable if it hadn't been for the appearance in town, one week before our departure, of Alex Lowe. He was on a tour for North Face, the outdoor clothing and equipment company that had been sponsoring him for several years. In the universe of climbing and exploration, Lowe had become a star of the first magnitude and you saw stories about him in *Outside* magazine, his picture in North Face advertisements, and articles and pictures in *Na-*

tional Geographic about some of his remarkable climbs. He was speaking and showing slides in the local high school gym on a Sunday night, one week before Brooke and I were leaving for South America.

Lowe spoke to a packed house. He looked terrific—lean and strong as a puma—and was wonderfully self-deprecating, describing Everest as a "sufferfest" (I'd heard that one before) and saying that hauling gear bags hundreds of feet up the side of a mountain in Antarctica was "sort of interesting."

He said that what he liked to do was go to interesting places and do things that are fun. Then he would show a slide of himself, hanging spectacularly off the smooth face of a huge rock wall somewhere, having already spent three of four days on the ascent.

"Now, *that's* fun," Lowe would smile and say when the audience gasped.

Most of the slides were of Lowe on some breathtaking climb. One, especially, caught my attention. Lowe has just leapt from a Zodiac, one of those inflatable boats, in the Antarctic Ocean and is beginning to climb an iceberg. His arms are fully extended above his head with the points of his axes buried. The front points of his crampons are also stuck into the ice. The bottoms of his boots are about three feet from the water. It is the sort of thing that Lowe could do. But, then, on ice or rock, no matter what the altitude, Alex Lowe could do just about anything.

Near the end of his talk, Lowe projected a picture of himself and his ten-year-old son onto the screen. The boy is in climbing gear, just like his dad, and when Lowe explained that this is an image of one of the best moments in his climbing life—he and Max are climbing the Grand, which they summited together—the audience applauded warmly.

After the talk, Lowe stood in the hall to shake hands and sign North Face posters that show him on an ice climb. Hadley,

Brooke, Marsha, and I waited in line and when it was our turn, I shook Lowe's hand and started to say something about how he probably didn't remember . . .

"Sure I do," he said. "You had a big birthday on the Grand."

Then he turned his attention and all of his considerable charm on Brooke, just as he had five years earlier, and asked her how she's been and if she was still doing any climbing. When she told him about Aconcagua, he said, "Great. Absolutely great. You two are going to have a wonderful time. Tell Jim Williams I said hello. He's terrific. And good luck. You'll do great."

Lowe was commonly called the world's greatest alpinist, but I thought he was also the world's greatest enthusiast. Just being around him gave you a pump. He signed a poster to all of us and I remembered again, as we stepped out in the cold night air, why I wanted to do this thing in the first place.

Teaming Up

Comradeship . . . is forged among high mountains, through the difficulties and dangers to which they expose those who aspire to climb them, the need to combine their efforts to attain their goal, the thrills of a great adventure shared together. — John Hunt, *The Ascent of Everest*

We had a Sunday plane out of JFK and Marsha insisted on driving us there. Hadley wanted to come along and keep her company on the long ride back home, but she was working on the lift at one of the local ski resorts. Sunday was one of their busy days and she couldn't get off. So on Saturday night we had a farewell dinner. We ate coq a vin and drank wine and told old family stories that made us laugh. Then we went to bed early, since it would be a long day for all of us.

Sunday morning finally, and time to leave. Brooke and I loaded two very heavy duffels and two slightly lighter packs into the trunk of Marsha's car.

"My God," she said when she watched us struggling with one of the duffels, "if it's that hard now, how are you going to get it up the mountain?"

I explained, sort of, that the duffel held gear that would only make it as far as base camp and that it would be carried there on the backs of mules. But I wondered myself.

▲ ▲ ▲

Marsha watched us unload the same gear at Kennedy, and when it was piled on the curb in front of the terminal said good-bye. She hugged Brooke and then me. Said good luck to both of us, smiled, and got back on the road for home. She'd had reservations about this climb all along, but she had never tried to talk me out of it. Hadn't said anything about how much she would worry. Hadn't done anything to dampen Brooke's spirits or mine. All of which, paradoxically, had made me feel even more selfish and guilty.

"You think she'll be okay?" Brooke said.

"She'll be fine," I said, "just as soon as we get back. Until then she'll worry."

I'd done the necessary things to cover myself. I had taken out the trip insurance and evacuation insurance, and I'd made sure the various wills, powers of attorney, and life insurance policies were current and located in a place where she could find them. I'd promised to call as soon as we got down off the mountain and I could find a phone.

Like millions of people who had read *Into Thin Air*, Marsha was aware of all the things that can go wrong in high-altitude mountaineering. When we'd talked about it, I said that I would turn around if I ever felt that going on would be dangerous. It was the right thing to say—and I certainly wasn't going to say the other thing—but it didn't really mean much as promises go. Those climbers on Everest probably felt the same way before they got up on the mountain, where suddenly success—meaning the summit—became a prize worth more suffering and greater risks than they could have ever imagined.

I had done all I could to reassure her and I honestly intended to be prudent without being timid. And I believed I could follow through on that because I had Brooke along.

▲　▲　▲

We flew to Miami, where we had a long layover. We passed the time in the American Airlines Admiral's Club (I fly a lot), where we watched the Super Bowl. While we were there, Marcus Allen came in and took a seat at the bar and watched the game with professional detachment.

"You know who that is?" I said to Brooke.

"No."

"Well, he starred in one of these things a few years ago. I think he still holds the record for the most yards gained in a Super Bowl by a running back."

"No kidding."

"Nope. And he had something to do with the O. J. case. I'm not sure what."

"I'd rather think of him as a football player."

The Falcons were out of it by the time our plane was called. We settled into the small seats. Took melatonin and tried to sleep. We flew all night and landed in Santiago around eight in the morning, as the city was coming to life.

We claimed our bags, got them through customs, and muscled them to a bus that took us into the city and the hotel where, according to the instructions we'd gotten from Jim Williams, we had a room waiting.

It was a small room. We stowed the duffels and Brooke had just turned the television to MTV to see how her Spanish was holding up when someone knocked on the door.

The man standing in the hall appeared to be in his young forties. He was tanned and looked athletic without being especially tall or muscular. He could have been a baseball player, perhaps, especially with the colorful muttonchop whiskers. But he had the eyes I had learned to look for and recognize. He was holding out his hand and I took it. We shook and he said, "Jim Williams. And you must be the Normans."

He had a good smile that stayed on his face for a while and a good grip. I liked him right away and said, "Come in."

He had some things to do, he said. But he would be back in

an hour or so. He'd go through our equipment with us then and make sure we had everything.

"If you don't," he said, "you *might* be able to find what you need here. Meanwhile, relax. Take a nap or," he said to Brooke, smiling and nodding at the television, "check out MTV."

When he came back for the equipment check, Williams was carrying a clipboard. He went down the list of items on a sheet of paper, reading off each piece of gear or clothing, which Brooke and I would find in our duffel and hold up for his inspection. He took his time. We had everything we needed.

He gave us his room number and said we could come up and get our lunch food whenever we wanted. Later in the day, he would get everyone on the climb together in the little courtyard of the hotel and give us a briefing. Then we would all go out to dinner. He looked like a man who had a lot of things to do but also the disposition to handle it. He seemed busy but not preoccupied or harassed.

Brooke and I packed everything back in our duffels and went upstairs to Williams' room. We met his assistant, Matt Goewert, a man of about 30 with blond hair, cut fairly long. He was tan and lean, agile and lithe, with a sweet, intelligent face. You could imagine him as one of those Californians who had been working on a degree in physics when he had been seduced away by something . . . climbing, surfing, motorcycles, Buddhism.

He was friendly and made jokes about the food he gave us in plastic bags. Salamis, cheeses, canned herring, candy bars, drink sweeteners, crackers.

"All your major food groups," he said. "A balanced diet is especially important at 19,000 feet when you are on your knees puking from the altitude."

We took the food back down to our room and packed it in the duffel like he had told us to. Then we took a nap.

▲　▲　▲

There were eight people sitting around a table in the little hotel courtyard when Brooke and I arrived. We recognized Jim Williams and Matt Goewert. The other six men were strangers who would become our teammates. They all looked to be in their early forties or, perhaps, late thirties. They were uniformly fit and they seemed, somehow, serious, as though this were a business meeting with some important money at stake.

The introductions were stiff but, then, they always are at first meetings like this. Everyone is holding back and, at the same time, trying to evaluate and make an impression. I tried to read faces as I shook hands and repeated names to help myself remember . . . Chris, Bob, Tom, Dave, Steve, Bob. They were, pretty clearly, all younger than I by 10 to 15 years. And they were all here for reasons they considered important, even if I didn't yet know what they were. (And I might not ever know.) But I guessed that they all had strong reasons, that none were here on a vagrant impulse. They would be motivated by something—a divorce, perhaps, or a career that had stalled or gone stale, or the realization that if you didn't start doing the things you had always dreamed of doing and told yourself you would do, and start doing them soon, then you would never do them.

I had been through these stiff first-night introductions in hunting and fishing lodges. But there had always been something lighthearted and casual about them. People generally tried not to come on too strong, to indicate that they looked at the week ahead as anything more than just another fishing trip. A chance to have some fun.

This was different. But then, climbing a big mountain was a large commitment. Of money and time, of course, but also something else that was more important than those things.

Which explained some of the looks Brooke and I got. Not hostile, exactly, but certainly probationary. These men were wondering what our presence among them would mean to the dynamic and the success of something they had a real stake in.

They were all here, unencumbered, and then this guy shows up with his young daughter. Would we hold them up? Keep them from the summit? Complain? Cramp their style? Turn into a general pain in the ass?

I tried to imagine how I would have felt at their ages and in their position, and I suspected I would have been a hard skeptic. I remembered back to that day in climbing school when Brooke had endured the spite of that instructor. I had the dismaying feeling that I had done it again. Only this time it was for three weeks, not one day.

Jim Williams spoke up and everyone quieted down and listened while he told us what to expect from the next couple of days. He answered some questions. Then he said he would lead the way to the restaurant where we would eat dinner.

▲ ▲ ▲

Brooke talked to Matt Goewert at dinner. He was closer than anyone at the table to her age, and it turned out that he had actually graduated from Berkeley with a degree in English. He was curious about the University of Chicago. They talked about books.

The rest of us talked about what we did for a living, where we lived, whatever climbing we had done. Brooke and I were, it seemed, the least-experienced members of the group. One man had climbed both Kilimanjaro and Denali, two of the seven summits. Another had done Denali. Another had climbed Rainier. Another, all the 14,000-foot peaks in Colorado where he lived.

The seafood at the restaurant was excellent. So was the Chilean wine and we all drank a lot of it. We were friendlier and more convivial, by far, when we left than we had been when we came in. Still, nobody except Matt had much to say to Brooke.

She didn't say anything about it before bed, but I knew it was on her mind.

▲ ▲ ▲

We loaded onto buses in the morning, with another group of climbers. There were three women clients in the group, and one of the guides was a woman from Seattle. I should have signed us up with that group, I thought. They were boisterous and seemed to have already coalesced as a team. We were still a collection of individuals. Six serious middle-aged men and then . . . me and Brooke.

It was a long ride, with a border crossing, to an Argentine ski resort that was closed for the season. We would eat dinner and spend the night there, in the base lodge hotel. Then, in the morning, we would begin our three-day trek into base camp.

The bus climbed slowly into the Andes along a series of switchbacks and the country became increasingly barren and harsh. We arrived at the ski resort in early afternoon. It had the forlorn look of any tourist operation in the off-season. We had a small room where the sheets and towels had been laundered so often they felt like tissue when you held them. The ski lifts looked like old derelict mining equipment left to rust.

Jim and Matt had work to do. Some of the men in our group went for a hike in the hills behind the resort. One or two of them napped. The rest of us helped Jim and Matt break down the food and other supplies for repacking in duffels that would be carried into base camp on the backs of mules. The idea was to pack according to when things would be needed and to break large containers down into smaller portions. Containers had to be sealed and labeled. Williams liked to cook and to eat as well as possible—in part, I suspect, because he had been climbing mountains for a long time and had eaten all the lentils, rice, chicken bouillon, freeze-dried ravioli, and other backcountry staples he could take. So we packed things like fresh lettuce, carrots, garlic, basil, and even eggs. This requires some special handling, which we took care of in what was probably the dining room of the resort.

It was pleasant work. Lots of busy hands and lots of conversation. It gave us a chance to learn something about Jim Williams.

The subject of the Everest debacle came up, which was probably inevitable. It is the lodestar topic for all climbing conversations. They all either start there or eventually come back around to it.

"I was there," Williams said.

"Where?" somebody asked.

"On Everest. I was at Camp Three, helping with the rescue."

It was equivalent, among people who climb or wish they did, to saying that you'd been in Dallas on November 22. Everyone in the room wanted to know more. Williams shrugged and sighed, as though to say he was tired of talking about it but knew there was no way he could avoid it.

Someone asked him if he thought it was the storm, if it would have happened if the weather hadn't turned?

"Everybody knows that you can run into bad weather on Everest," Williams said. "That's not news. And as storms go up there, that one wasn't especially bad."

Then, was it because the climbers were inexperienced?

Williams looked around at the people helping him. "How many of you are expert climbers?" he said. "A lot of expert climbers have died on Everest and a lot of novice climbers have made it to the summit. And you need to remember that three of the people who died in that thing were guides, and two of them were the expert guides."

"What about Sandy Pittman?" somebody said.

"What about her?" Williams answered.

"Well, wasn't she being short roped by one of the Sherpas?"

"So what? That's a common technique. She made it to the summit with the rest of her team. People want to make her the heavy. Sandy wasn't responsible for what happened up there."

"Do you know her?"

"I was her guide when she started this seven summits thing. Guided her up Aconcagua, in fact."

"What happened?"

"She fired me."

Nobody asked why but the question, of course, hung on the stale air of the big room, so Williams answered it.

"I was willing to be her guide but I wasn't willing to be her servant. Sandy's different. She's very demanding and she needs to be the center of whatever scene she's in. But she made her way up the mountain and she wasn't responsible for what happened up there."

After an awkward pause, the conversation went on. Williams plainly believed that the guides who had died on Everest made mistakes that were motivated by a desire to get high-profile clients to the top. Pittman was sending back dispatches to a Web site and Jon Krakauer was along, on assignment for *Outside*. He had no idea, of course, that he would witness the seminal event in modern mountaineering and write about it in a book that would become both a best-seller and a classic in the literature of adventure.

"All that raised the stakes and made those guides do things they might not have done otherwise," Williams said. It was a severe judgment but it was not rendered harshly. The men had made mistakes that seemed small when they made them, and they had paid a heavy price.

"You get fixed on the summit," Williams said, almost sorrowfully. "That happens anyway. And it's probably a stronger feeling under those kind of circumstances. But you have to get past that. I had a client once, an Englishwoman, who was 300 feet from the summit of Everest, but I could tell from the way she was moving and the amount of oxygen she had already used, that she was going to reach the summit late and she wasn't going to have any gas on the descent. So I turned her around."

Three hundred feet from the summit.

And what made the story more remarkable was this: Williams, who is a world-class climber and guide, had never, in five tries, made it to the summit of Everest himself. That was his own best chance. Three hundred feet from the summit. He could have told his client to wait for him, that he would be back in a minute, and bagged the summit on his own. One of the guides who died in 1996 had pushed on for the summit after all of his clients had made it and were on the way down. Williams plainly thought this was not merely a mistake. It was also un-professional, which was worse.

"He wasn't there to get to the summit. He'd already done that, anyway, on another climb. His job was to make sure his clients got to the summit—which they'd done—and then got down. He forgot what he was there to do."

A couple of the people in the room looked at the floor in silent disagreement or, perhaps, because they thought this was speaking a little too harshly of the dead. Easier, more secure to blame Sandy Pittman and the espresso machine and laptop she made her Sherpas carry up from base camp.

▲ ▲ ▲

We worked most of the afternoon, and when the bags were all packed and ready to be loaded on the mules, Brooke and I went back to our little room to clean up and rest for a few minutes.

"Well," I said, "I feel like we're in good hands, anyway."

"Yeah," Brooke said, "Sandy Pittman's guide. You can't do much better than that."

"Three hundred feet from the summit and he turned the client around," I said. "I like that."

Starting at the Bottom

I have this day ascended the highest mountain in this district. . . . I have cherished this project for many years.
— Petrarch

I woke up early, when Brooke had some kind of nightmare, and I watched the gathering sun through the smeared glass of the window in our little room. I was apprehensive but still happy that we were here. More worried for Brooke than myself. I thought back to other nights when I'd listened, through my own sleep, for sounds of her distress, of times when Marsha and I had comforted her after bad dreams and earaches. She went back to sleep on her own, this morning, with no help from me.

The other group of climbers—the one that included some women—left the ski lodge before we did. They had been animated and loud, even though they'd been a "team" only as long as our group. Things seemed a little dispirited once they had gone. We sat outside and made desultory conversation while we waited for the trucks that would take us a few miles down the road to the trailhead where we were starting our trek to base camp and, from there, our climb of Aconcagua.

Finally, it was our turn and we loaded packs and ourselves into a Land Cruiser that belonged to a man Williams had hired for this job and to provide mules and other services, including helping with permits. He made a living at it and had his business logo printed on the Toyota's doors. I talked, on the way to the trail, with one of the men on our team, about how the American craze for adventure sports had provided an economic boost for remote places around the world.

"They probably think we're crazy," the man said, "and hope to God we don't get over it."

The man who drove the Toyota helped us unload our packs and solemnly shook hands with each of us, wishing us good luck, before we started down the trail.

▲ ▲ ▲

Less than an hour after we'd started, a beaten climber passed us, going the other way on the back of the mule and muttering about how he couldn't make it, he just couldn't make it. If I saw it as an omen, none of the other climbers in our group paid any attention, including Brooke. We moved up a trail that ran next to a river swollen with cloudy glacial melt and our pace was steady and fast, as though we had been caged these last few days and were glad to be moving at last.

We stayed together at first, but after an hour or so we began to spread out along the trail. Brooke stayed close to the head of the pack, then dropped back toward the middle. Some of the men in our group were making a point of what kind of pace they could set. I was at the end, moving at my own speed, and remembering what Joe Lentini had told me as we were leaving North Conway.

"Don't leave it all on the trek in," I told myself. "Save something for the summit."

▲ ▲ ▲

We were hidden from the high mountains in this river valley. It was hot and the country around us was harsh and, except for the dirty river water, arid. I wore shorts and sneakers and I was quickly damp with sweat. It could have been a high desert hike.

"Drink plenty of water and use plenty of sunscreen," Williams said when we took a break.

"Do you realize," Brooke said, "that we've been told that by some of the greatest climbers in the world?"

We arrived at that night's camp a little before sunset. It had been about a ten-mile walk and not especially strenuous. Brooke volunteered to help fill water jugs for Williams, who set up to cook as soon as the mules arrived. On the way back to the stream some of the gauchos who were driving the mules whistled at her and shouted, "*Rubia.*"

"*Es solamente pelo,*" she said, and they laughed.

After we had our tent up, we helped Williams, peeling and slicing carrots and then tossing a salad. Bent in concentration over a little gas stove, he made pasta and pesto sauce with fresh basil and garlic. We ate hungrily and we drank wine but not as much, by far, as we had in Santiago. A couple of swallows each, maybe, but it was a Williams touch to bring wine along to base camp. And we all appreciated it The other group ate lentils and rice and drank Kool-Aid.

The air turned cold enough, after the sun went down, to feel like we were in the mountains. Otherwise, it did not seem much like a climbing expedition. We still hadn't seen anything that even looked like big, daunting mountains. Just scrappy little hills guarding the flanks of a river.

"You doing okay?" I said to Brooke after we'd drifted off to our tent. We could hear the other people in our group. They were still up, shivering in the cold, telling their various stories, laughing, and watching the stars come out.

"Sure," she said, "fine."

The other clients in the group had been cordial enough, all day, but nobody had made much of an effort to talk to her. But then, they were all old enough to be her father, and when one of them did talk to her, there was something awkward and nervous about it. Those conversations were inevitably abrupt, and I suppose, if you were Brooke you could read them as rude.

I understood, and sympathized . . . both with Brooke and the men on our climb. I wasn't usually so tolerant, but when I considered it, I realized that while I could talk easily enough with Brooke about many things, conversation with her friends was just about impossible. I would have had the same problem the other men were having if I'd come here by myself and one of them had brought his daughter along. I thought about explaining this to Brooke but didn't. But I hoped that, with time, the other men would begin to see her as a teammate and not as a kid. And, I thought, it could happen. For now, none of us thought of each other as teammates—or of ourselves as a team.

And, anyway, Brooke wasn't complaining.

"I guess we'll get a look at the mountain tomorrow," I said.

"Yep."

"Well, good night."

"Good night, Dad."

I lay awake for a while, trying to get comfortable, seeing the mental afterimage of that beaten man on the mule, and thinking, *what have I gotten us into?*

▲ ▲ ▲

We started early the next morning while there was still mist pooling in the low ground around the river. We had a longer walk ahead of us today, Williams had said, but it would not be especially hard. He reminded us to drink plenty of water and wear lots of sunscreen, and Brooke wondered, under her breath, where she had heard *that* before.

We were quickly spread out along the trail, Jim and three of the clients setting a quick, steady pace. Then two of the men coming along behind them followed by Brooke and then me. A big, gruff man named Tom was making a video of the climb with some experimental 3-D equipment his company had developed. He was moving up and down the trail. Matt was following along behind everyone. Not because he was slow, certainly, but because he was the assistant guide and that was where he belonged.

By mid-morning, I was working harder than I had expected to. Not struggling, exactly, but exerting myself more than if I had been on an all-day hike back home in Vermont. I seemed to need more air than I could get by breathing normally. I was sweating and panting and feeling the weight of my fairly light pack. It had to be the altitude, I thought. We were at 9,000 feet or so and gaining 1,000 feet a day. I was not, I decided, fully acclimatized.

If I was merely having difficulty, Brooke was struggling. She dropped behind me and when I stopped to wait for her, she said, "No, Dad, go on. Please. I'll be all right."

"You're sure?"

"Yes," she said, breathing hard and fast, like she just could not get enough air, "go on. I'll catch up."

I moved on down the trail, at my own slow pace, wondering if we would even make it through the second day and get as far as base camp. A retreat now might be in the cards and it would be truly ignominious.

It had to be the altitude, I thought. I knew that she was trying and that she was in shape. She simply might not have the physiology for high-altitude climbing, and for that matter, I might not, either. We might have to stay with rock climbing at low altitudes and bail out on my dream—or perhaps it was a fantasy—of "one big climb." By late morning, I was trudging along in gloom. Brooke was half a mile behind me, and every time I turned around to check on her, she seemed to be stopped and bent over the ski poles we all used for balance. I began to wonder if we might have to find a mule to get her back to the highway.

At midday, I caught up with the rest of the group, sitting in the shade of a high ledge along the riverbank, opening packs and picking out something for lunch. I looked back at Brooke, moving slowly across a wide flat, dried floodplain of rock and sand. It was hot and the air above the ground shimmered so she seemed to be moving through water, coming in and out of focus. She looked very small and feeble.

I dropped my pack and went back to help her.

"No, Dad," she said when I got to her, "I can make it. I'll carry my pack."

"Just give it to me," I said. "I'd do the same even if you weren't my daughter."

Which was persuasive, even if it didn't make sense. I took her pack and shouldered it and we walked in together.

When she dropped to the ground in the shade, somebody said, "You okay, Brooke?" It was said with kindness, which might have been worse than if it had been meant as a taunt. One thing to be the only woman in the group and the youngest. Something else to be the kid.

"I'm okay," she said, sounding curt even through her exhaustion.

Williams came over and knelt down beside her.

"Here," he said, and handed her his water bottle. He had mixed some kind of juice. "Drink this."

"I'm okay."

"Go on," he said, "drink it."

Brooke's skin had the pale, damp, and clammy look that comes with heat exhaustion. Her breathing was shallow and her lips were white. She was wearing a dark polypropylene top like the defeated climber we had seen riding the mule on his way out. Williams asked her if she had anything lighter.

She shook her head.

"I've got something," I said, and got a white shirt I wore on the bonefish flats out of my pack.

I gave her the shirt and Williams said, "That's better. Now how about a hat?"

"I didn't bring one," Brooke said.

Williams shook his head, as though to say *Clients*.

"I've got a spare," one of the other climbers said. A man named Dave, who was quiet and friendly and turned out to be the strongest climber in the group. But that would become clear later. This morning he was having troubles of his own. He was limping.

He gave Brooke a long-billed hat and a bandana, which Williams helped her rig so that it covered the back of her neck. Williams also gave her some extra-strength sunblock. "You're already getting burned," he said. "You've got to use this stuff. The higher we get, the more important it will be."

She nodded and accepted a water bottle from one of the other climbers. "This will replace those electrolytes," he said. He was an oil geologist by profession and he had brought an utterly scientific approach to this climb. He knew all the physiological responses to altitude by name. He knew the medications and how they worked. He monitored his pulse and respiration like a physician with a critical patient. I'd spent as much time in conversation with him as anyone in the group and I enjoyed his company. He had been almost courtly to Brooke.

She drank and thanked him.

One of the other men refilled her water bottle, and she also thanked him. If having Brooke around cramped their style and made them self-conscious, it didn't keep them from being supportive and helpful. They were still strangers to me, but they were also, I thought, good guys . . . and better than that.

While Williams and the others were looking after Brooke, I asked Dave about his limp.

"New boots," he said, sounding slightly embarrassed. "I think I've got a blister."

"I've got tape," I said, eager to help and repay a kindness. "Right in my first-aid kit."

"Do you mind?"

"Come on," I said, and went into my pack.

Dave took off his boots. He had rubbed the skin off a spot on his heel. It was the size of a bottle top. There was a flap, then a raw red place.

"Oh, man," I said and cut a strip of tape.

Williams watched and said, "New boots?" Like he knew this drill from a hundred other times.

"Yes," Dave said sheepishly. Everyone knows what new boots can do, and he was not a rookie.

"I can't believe it," Williams said. "What size are you?"

"Ten and a half."

"Okay," Williams said, unlacing his boots, "trade with me."

"I can't do that."

"What else are you going to do? You can't walk to base camp barefoot. Come on, give me your boots and put these on."

Williams' boots were a half size larger than Dave's, which he jammed his own feet into, leaving the laces very loose.

"Nice and snug," he said. "Perfect fit."

"Now, that," a man named Bob Gutherie said, "is a guide who will do a little extra. Serve you wine on the approach and give you the boots off his own feet."

Something about the gesture gave everyone a pump.

Including Brooke, who had eaten lunch—some cheese and some sausage and a Power Bar. Her pack was full of them, mostly banana, her favorite flavor. She seemed to get stronger on the trail that afternoon, and I said something to Williams, during a break, about the wonderful recuperative powers of youth.

"Yeah," he said. "I seem to remember."

Brooke made it to camp easily, walking near the head of our

group. We had passed our first crisis, one that would shrink to laughable insignificance in the coming days.

▲ ▲ ▲

Our second camp was on a cool grassy flat, with a clear stream flowing through it. Climbers from our group and two or three others that were using the site bathed, shampooed, and washed clothes in the clear, cold water. But the best part of the site was the view of the mountain.

You saw it down a river valley flanked by small mountains that formed an almost perfect V, like a gun sight. Aconcagua sat squarely in these sights, entirely filling the V. When you looked in that direction, you could not see anything except the massive white mountain. It seemed to demand your entire focus and attention, and you knew that if you were not a strict rationalist, you would believe devoutly that gods or spirits lived there and that the mountain itself could be wrathful. The Incas, in fact, may have been the first to summit Aconcagua. In the 1930s, climbers found mummified Inca remains above 15,000 feet, where the terrain is so bleak and inhospitable, no one would go there unless it was to climb . . . or to speak to the gods.

Doing the busy work of camp—pitching a tent, unrolling sleeping bags, helping with dinner—I could not go very long without looking down the valley at the looming, formidable profile of that mountain. There are, I suppose, people who do not find mountains compelling, who would have been able to resist that view, but I could not imagine it.

Brooke noticed me staring, hypnotically, at the mountain.

"Think you can handle it, Dad?" she said playfully.

"I don't know," I said. "Looks to me like that is one heavy hill."

She laughed. It was an old family joke. When she was two and not very experienced at walking, we had been on a beach and Brooke started up a steep dune with soft sand. It was hard-going on short legs, and halfway up she turned and said to me, with the wonderful seriousness of a child trying to make adult conversation, "DaDa, this is a *heavy* hill." The line had been part of the family inventory ever since.

We watched the mountain as we talked. The sun went down and Aconcagua began to glow, as though lit by some internal fire, until it was the pure, rich orange of the sun rising fresh out of the sea.

"I don't think there is a word for that," Brooke said, "now that they've ruined 'awesome.' "

I agreed. The mountain continued glowing long after the sun was down. Brooke and I sat up watching it and talking about things. We zipped our fleece jackets and kept talking as the air turned cold and the sky went dark and then began collecting stars until there were hundreds, maybe thousands. Brooke had been reading *War and Peace* and she had a lot of things to say about that book. I could remember being her age and feeling that way about a book. For me, it had been *Absalom, Absalom.* We talked about Tolstoy's notions of fate and free will, which is the kind of conversation that, in most other settings, would have required heavy seasoning with irony, skepticism, and hip superiority. None of that was necessary here. It occurred to me, after we had said good night and were in our sleeping bags, that if nothing else came from this climb and we never got close to the summit, this evening was something I'd always be grateful for.

Base Camp Blues

*Close to the sun in lonely lands
Ringed by the azure world.*
　　　　　　　—Tennyson

The next afternoon, we reached base camp. It was as squalid and harsh as the camp downstream had been pastoral and serene. Now that we were actually on Aconcagua, the mountain did not seem at all beautiful. We were too high for vegetation to grow and too low for snow and ice at this time of year. Our environment, then, was all rock, gravel, and a kind of fine, powdery dirt that the wind seemed to gather and keep suspended on the air so that when you breathed through your mouth, you found your teeth and tongue coated with a layer of grit like fine sandpaper.

And if the terrain here was inhospitable in its natural state, the presence of humans made it worse.

At roughly the center of the wide plateau, which was base camp, there was a small, semi-permanent shelter that the park rangers used as a headquarters. There was a small antennae farm for the radios and a couple of plywood and canvas latrines that were so foul almost nobody used them. You could not dig a deep enough hole to accommodate the volume of waste, and evidently, the altitude was not congenial to the kind of microbes that break it down. Behind every boulder, you saw evidence of other climbers who had used this place as an alternative to those nasty latrines. Now and then the wind would catch a sheet of toilet paper and blow it through base camp. Nobody seemed to be collecting litter.

There were clusters of tents all over base camp and the vivid colors of Mountain Hardware, the North Face, and Marmot looked gaudily out of place in the bleakly monochromatic setting.

Brooke studied the little clusters of ornamental tents, appraising what they did for the landscape. "Like putting a party dress on a pig," she said.

The group that we'd been with since Santiago had taken another route to the summit, so the only climber any of us knew at base camp was a young Polish man who was going up Aconcagua alone, as a way of training for an Everest expedition he hoped to join. He was friendly and very strong, making two trips to every campsite because he had so much gear and hadn't hired a mule.

"Probably doesn't have the money," somebody on our team said.

"Have you seen what he eats?" someone else said in tones of disbelief.

We all became friendly with the man, though no one seemed to be able to catch, or pronounce, his name. So he became "the Polish kid." Williams, typically, had packed a tent large enough to hold our entire team and in which we could all stand comfortably. The communal tent was where we ate and generally hung out while we were at base camp. We invited the Polish kid for dinner. He seemed reluctant, almost as though we were living too lavishly and that by joining us, he would somehow be breaking training. But he did eat with us once.

Williams was cooking extravagantly. Using the fresh eggs, for example, to make huevos rancheros for breakfast one morning. So on our day of rest, anyway, our team was having a fine time at base camp.

But the word among other climbers was that things were bad up near the summit. Brooke and I talked to a couple from Colorado while we were down at the communal water source, filling bottles. The woman was the picture of Rocky Mountain vitality. Tall and obviously fit, with dazzling blonde hair and gleaming white teeth, she looked like she could have been paid to model the North Face parka she was wearing. She had failed to make the summit.

"I just felt so sick at camp two," she said. "They thought I might have an edema."

That was at a little over 17,000 feet. Her boyfriend, who looked, if anything, like more of a natural climber than she, had come down with her. He'd developed a cough that made it hard to breathe even when he was standing still.

"We've done a lot of climbing at home," he said, "but we weren't ready for this altitude."

Still, they seemed oddly sanguine. But that made more sense once they explained that the rest of their group was trapped in tents at 19,000 feet, unable to summit because of the weather.

"You can see how hard it's blowing," the man said and pointed to the false summit of Aconcagua, high above us, obscured by a white plume of snow, whipped up by the wind.

"We've talked to them on the radio. They say it's blowing about 80 with gusts of 100. This is their fifth day in the tents and they're almost out of food. If it doesn't break tomorrow, they're coming down."

It was a sobering encounter. I had my image of the defeated climber on the back of the mule; now Brooke could imagine herself as the blonde with the straight white teeth who gave out at 17,500.

▲ ▲ ▲

We spent our rest day at base camp. This was supposed to help us acclimatize; however, I didn't feel like I was making much progress in that department. Just walking a few hundred yards back to my tent from the water point, which was a very slight incline, left my chest burning. I would stop to rest and look up at the route we would be taking the next day and wonder, not if I could make it, but if I had any chance at all.

I despised the idea of not making it. You hate that under any terms but with Brooke as my partner, it seemed especially painful. A part of me wanted to confide my fears to her, but that was insupportable. This was my daughter. I had calmed her down and taken care of her after she turned over a nest of angry yellow jackets and helped her through all kinds of other crises. She had always believed in me. "You can do anything," I remember her saying once, when she was little and we were working on some kind of backyard project.

I couldn't imagine surrendering whatever was left of that status in her imagination. Not without a fight.

But she wasn't a kid anymore and she was on to my mood. She no doubt saw me staring at the climbers who'd already had their rest day and were moving out of base camp and up the mountain, growing smaller and smaller, until they appeared antlike before they vanished around a cornice. She knew what I was thinking but was wise enough not to approach the subject directly.

So she talked to me about other, inconsequential things. We talked about family trips to New Orleans and New York. Dogs and cats that had been with us at one time or another. Friends back in Vermont. I was reminded of long car trips, years earlier, when there was nothing like the sound of my kids' voices and their palpable enthusiasm to get my mind off whatever was bothering me and raise my spirits. It worked back then and it worked now. The difference back then was that Brooke hadn't been aware of the effect the sound of her voice had on me. She knew what she was doing here. She probably did not realize that I was on to her. And very grateful.

Five days after we had started down the trail, we left base camp wearing plastic mountain boots and carrying full packs. This was the first carry and for me, it was an ordeal. When you imagine yourself on a mountain, climbing, you move from situations that are dangerous to those that are sublime. In your mind, it is all risk and poetry. But when you are actually there, you spend most of your time humping a load. We were going to climb Aconcagua the way most climbers do most big mountains, by setting up a series of camps above base camp. We would "carry high," and "sleep low." Each carry to a new camp would gain us a couple of thousand feet of altitude. Our last camp, before we tried for the summit would be at just over 19,000 feet. Between there and base camp, for ten days, we would be carrying loads, setting up and breaking down camps, and occasionally resting.

The first carry, to 15,600 feet, took me all day. I was the last person to make it to the site of our next camp and cache food and fuel and other things I would not need for the night. Brooke did better, even though she struggled, too. At one point, near the end of the carry, we had to make our way through a large field of very soft snow. If you put your foot in the wrong spot, you would sink to your waist or deeper and then have to posthole your way for a few steps until you found better footing. My pack was not as heavy as it might have been. Fifty pounds, maybe. But it seemed to drive me down into the soft snow and then to pull me back when I tried to go forward. The sun was bright and hot, beating down on the mountain from a clear sky that was as blue as a jewel. I was sweating like a man in a sauna as I struggled through the snow.

Brooke and I went back down together. It was almost dark by the time we reached the big communal dining tent. We ate without much appetite. The other climbers were also tired but seemed to be in better spirits than we were. I left for my own tent and sleeping bag almost as soon as I finished eating. Brooke stayed around awhile. Tomorrow was a rest day, and as I zipped myself into my bag, I was grateful for that, anyway.

▲ ▲ ▲

The next morning, Jim Williams spoke to Brooke, me, and the other climber in our group who planned on going up the Polish Glacier route.

"You saw what it was like yesterday," he said. "It's going to be like that on the Polish. Maybe not quite as bad because it's higher. But it is also going to be harder climbing because of the increased altitude. I think you ought to bag the glacier, leave your harnesses and helmets in your duffels with the gear that goes off on the mules. It's going to be hard enough getting up the *Ruta Normal*." He was speaking to all of us, but he was looking at me when he said this.

None of us argued with him.

After a rest day, we broke down the big tent and sent everything that was not going with us to the summit, down on mules. We wouldn't see any of it until we got back to the ski lodge. I had cut my load as much as I thought possible for the next carry to the site where we had cached our gear.

It was another hard day. Not quite as hard, perhaps, as the first carry. This time, I stayed out of the snowfield. But the trail we took was covered with loose rock and it gave way, sliding under your foot when you took a step so that sometimes it felt like you were taking two steps forward and one back.

It was another long day.

Brooke did better than I. She seemed to be getting stronger. On the day after the second carry, she made another carry while I had to rest. Maybe, I thought, she was acclimatizing better than I. Or, probably, it was because she was 30 years younger than I and could bounce back on one night's rest.

Whatever the reason, she was not the struggling, complaining teenager she had been that first day on the Grand. She was one of the grown-ups, carrying her share and probably mine as well. I wasn't sure how I felt about that.

When she came down after that carry, she asked me how I was doing. I felt myself resenting it. I was supposed to be looking after her. But Williams had told me not to make the carry, had turned me around when I tried. I told myself I could have made it and then told myself not to be a baby—there would be more carries.

And there were.

Brooke and I made them all, but we struggled. We suffered from headaches, racking coughs, nosebleeds, diminished appetites, sleeplessness combined with fatigue, and probably some others that I have forgotten.

By the time we made our second high camp, I was clearly the weakest member of our group. Finishing every carry an hour or two behind everyone else. Wondering how much longer it would be before I would be forced into an ungraceful surrender and retreat on the back of a mule. Still, Brooke and I managed to keep going. When we established the new camp, we had to pitch our tent in a high wind. Once we had it up, we had to anchor it with rocks, some the size of basketballs. We'd lift the rocks from wherever we found them and carry them to the tent site, staggering a little with the weight and because our legs were still rubbery from the climbing. We tied the tent down to the rock and then stopped for a minute, bent over at the waist, hands on knees, and gasped wildly for air. When we were breathing again in what passed for a normal fashion, we went off to find more rocks.

It took an hour to set up a simple tent, then get everything inside and arranged for the night. And these routine jobs got harder as we got higher on the mountain.

Unsurprisingly, some people in our group had an easier time

with altitude than others. Jim Williams and Matt Goewert operated always like they were at sea level. Matt would sometimes skip up the mountain, in his big plastic boots, singing. Williams moved fluidly, without show, keeping an eye on his clients, always the leader.

The rest of us were straining. But as the altitude increased so did our cohesion. We had started out as a group of paying clients, only one or two of whom knew each other, and through the alchemy of this climb, we were starting to resemble a team. This showed itself mostly in the way we extended little courtesies to each other.

"I'm going for water," someone would say, "want me to fill your bottles?"

If you had an ailment—something small like a blister—someone would offer you a strip of moleskin from his first-aid kit. There were always volunteers to do the little communal chores. Which might seem like no big deal at sea level but in the extremes of altitude, where everyone is struggling to some degree, you would expect to see more selfishness and less altruism.

As we stayed longer and climbed higher on the mountain, the rest of the group seemed to accept Brooke increasingly as just one of the guys. She carried her loads and she did not complain, and the men on the team talked to her as an equal.

In communal moments, usually at mealtimes, you tried to hold up your end with stories, and everyone in our group had good ones. About oil exploration in the bayous of Louisiana, about Peace Corps work in Africa, about playing football for the University of Miami, and about a collision with a cow on a motorcycle ride down the Baja. Brooke held her own at these moments, telling stories about life on the South Side of Chicago or about going to the bullfights when she had been studying abroad, in Barcelona.

So, without having to work at it, we became friendly and

then friends and even something like teammates. And I felt a lot of gratitude when I would come out of my tent at one of the high camps and see Brooke talking and sometimes laughing with one or two of the men in the group. The initial skepticism was gone, left behind with a lot of other gear at base camp.

High Camps, Hard Times

Ecstasy, I thought, is found in the brief resting time be-
tween the effort of the exploring body and the sterner
mental effort that awaits.
　　　　　—Wilfred Noyce, Climbing the Fish's Tail

In ten days of carrying loads, setting up camps, and then breaking down camps, my universe shrank. I was like a monk and the mountain was my monastery. The little jobs—packing and repacking—were my devotionals, and when I put one foot laboriously in front of the other, I might have been chanting. I began to feel a kind of intimacy with this mountain and a fondness for the different colors of its rocks and the way the light played off them. It was especially good to look back down at where we had been, and feel this sense of having put something—many things—behind you.

When we'd left Kennedy Airport, Bill Clinton was being tried for high crimes and misdemeanors by the United States Senate and that seemed like a crucial moment in history. Up here, it was hard to give a rat's ass. Nobody talked about it. Instead, we told each other stories about other climbs, motorcycle trips, and bullfights in Barcelona. Brooke was reading Conrad in her sleeping bag. I'd brought Hemingway's short stories. We talked about those books before we went to sleep. It all seemed a little cleaner up here and I didn't miss Jim

Lehrer, the *New York Times*, or any of that. However things turned out for Brother Bill, it didn't seem especially important at 17,500 feet. I much preferred to listen to Jim Williams talk about skiing to the South Pole or tell stories about how Alex Lowe, who was a friend, was known on an expedition for two signature lines—"Mind if I go ahead?" and "See you back at camp."

We were into the cold and the wind at that altitude, but nothing serious. We were still on schedule. There had been rest days but we hadn't been trapped in our tents by weather. So far, the climb had been arduous, but benign. Nobody was complaining. Still . . . I think many of us must have wondered, is this all there is?

The wind was strong and building, and there were clouds when we made our move to 19,000. It was a long walk, and since we were all moving at different speeds, our group was quickly strung out across the mountain. I was, as usual, at the end of the line. Brooke was a couple of hundred yards ahead of me. I could not see the climbers at the head of the line. No problem, I thought, it was a clear trail. We would find our way.

About halfway across a vast moraine, the snow started falling. At first, it was no more than a nuisance—not flakes so much as ugly little gobs of cold slush, like frozen spit, that stung your exposed skin and smeared your glasses. But the temperature also seemed to be falling and the wind was definitely picking up. I pulled the hood of my parka over my head and snugged it.

In an hour, the tentative squall had become a full storm and we were in blizzard conditions. I could not see Brooke even when she was just twenty or thirty feet ahead of me. We had both gone into our packs and switched from glacier glasses to goggles and put on balaclavas to cover the last exposed skin around our faces and necks. The snow was accumulating rapidly on the trail, making it both hard to find and difficult to keep your footing. I stopped to put on crampons and had trouble working the straps. It took awhile and by the time I got the crampons properly fitted and put my shell gloves back on, my hands were very cold.

I kept walking. Struggling not merely with the thin air but with the wind, the snow, and the poor visibility, a combination of forces that seemed to leech the energy from my body. Walking had been hard before; now it became an act of desperation and whatever rhythm I had established up to now was gone entirely. I was flailing, like a kid in deep snow, dragging his sled. Except my mom wasn't here.

My daughter was, however, and when I could make out her shape ahead of me, I could see that she was struggling, too. A sense of apprehension—not quite panic, yet—began rising inside me. It isn't necessary to have read all the literature of climbing, just one or two books, to know about storms at altitude and what they can do to climbers. I remembered a footnote from *K2: The Savage Mountain* about a man named Richard Burdsall who had been one of the finest American big mountain climbers and had died, on this very mountain, in a storm in 1953. In some dark, oxygen-starved part of my brain, I began to imagine the worst. And as bad as the worst was, some of the alternatives seemed just as bad. Severe frostbite? The kind that results in amputations? The idea of my little girl maimed was too ugly to contemplate . . . but I did, for a minute or two.

Then I made myself do what you should always do in a situation like that. I stopped, did some breathing, and gathered it up.

When I was thinking clearly—and moving—again, I told myself that somewhere up ahead of us was one of the finest climbers and guides in the world and no matter how bad the storm got, he wasn't going to let us stay out and bivouac in it. It seemed important that I share this reassuring thought with Brooke.

When I caught up with her, she was sitting on a rock, tired and resting. I had to shout so she could hear me over the wind.

Her expression was hidden by the goggles and the balaclava. But the tone, when she said, "Sure. Everything's cool," was clear and reassuring.

But not as reassuring as Jim Williams' profile, which appeared in the swirling mist, a few minutes later. He was smiling, like we had just bumped into each other on the street somewhere and, "Hey, how about a cup of coffee?"

"How you doing?" he shouted.

"Jake," I said.

He took Brooke's pack and they walked ahead into camp, then he came back for me.

Things at camp were not so good. One man was bent over, throwing up on his boots, and another was sitting on a rock, numbed and disoriented. Everyone else was working to get the tents up. Brooke was shoveling snow to clear a place for our tent. I dropped my pack and worked with her, shoveling; threading aluminum tent poles through small nylon loops with numbed and gloved fingers, a job that seemed something like trying to thread a needle while wearing mittens; holding the tent down in the gale force winds; finding the rocks to secure it. It seemed like awfully hard work and to go very slowly. One pair from our group had so much trouble, they eventually gave up and crowded in with other climbers, making two-man tents into three-man tents.

Finally, Brooke and I had it done and were in our sleeping bags. She could not get warm and was shuddering uncontrollably. I was worried enough to put my boots back on and walk out into the storm, to the tent where Jim and Matt were melting snow for the water they would need to cook supper.

"She's dehydrated," Jim said. "Tell her to drink lots of water. And tea when we bring it around."

A few minutes later, Matt unzipped our tent and said in a lilting voice, "Room service. Someone called for tea?"

This seemed somehow almost unbearably funny and for the first time in hours, Brooke and I laughed. We laughed for a long time, and kept laughing between sips of our wonderfully hot tea until we were too tired to laugh anymore.

The morning was clear and still, with the sky so blue it hurt your eyes. We rested and reorganized. While the stronger people in our group went down the mountain to bring up some food and cooking gas we had cached, I melted snow to fill water bottles and alternated between admiring the view and brooding. I was at 19,000 feet, looking down on things I could never have imagined seeing from this perspective.

We were at the base of the Polish Glacier, a 3,000-foot wall of ice that rose above us to the summit ridge. We watched as a pair of climbers made their arduous way up the face of the Polish. They looked very small and it didn't seem likely they would make it. Another climber told us about a man who had fallen, a few days earlier, from nearly the top of the glacier all the way to where we were sitting.

"They had to evacuate him, of course. He was pretty busted up," the man said. "Miracle he survived at all."

Because we were making such good time, we had more food than we needed—or wanted—to carry. So we spread tins of herring, whole sausages, cheese wrapped in foil, and various kinds of chocolate—on a plastic sheet and invited other climbers to a buffet lunch. The only condition was—if you ate something, you also had to take some away with you.

We had lots of takers. One team especially had been on the mountain for a long time and hadn't been well provisioned to start with. One man from that team ate two tins of herring before he even looked up to talk.

His first words were, "You want to pass me some of that cheese. And a package of that chocolate."

We got rid of a lot of food.

Which was fine with me. I had pretty much lost my appetite. But Jim Williams was still trying to cook interesting food—we had some kind of rice seasoned with saffron, among other things, at 19,000 feet. And he certainly was not losing his appetite. Brooke and I watched him in awe when he found a frozen onion in one of the food bags, cut it in half, scooped a little cavity from the center, and then filled it with the last of his mayonnaise, which was also frozen. He put the onion in his mouth and chewed like a man in pure contentment.

▲ ▲ ▲

I not only couldn't eat much, I also felt like I was growing weaker and that my body had done about all the acclimatizing it was going to do. My morale was good—I was genuinely happy to be where I was—but I was deteriorating physiologically. Not as drastically as a woman in another group, who showed signs of serious disorientation. She was taken down at the insistence of Jim Williams, who recognized the symptoms of a cerebral edema. I wasn't breaking down dramatically, like that—merely wearing out, like my old Ford truck. I saw myself, with depressing clarity, as that man riding a mule out and saying, "I couldn't make it. I just couldn't make it."

Brooke, however, was still strong and getting stronger. She had gone back down the mountain to help bring up the cached stuff. She was busy around the camp. She wasn't the strongest person in our group, but there didn't seem much doubt that she would make it to the summit.

I needed to have a talk with her, I decided. The kind of talk that you have a lot, but never get used to having, I suppose, when you are a dad. The kind where you say things that have to be said but that you wish you didn't have to talk about. I decided, as I had many times, to put the talk off as long as possible.

We had one last carry. It was a traverse, not a climb, to put us in a better position to go for the summit. While nothing is exactly easy at 19,000 feet, this shouldn't have been as hard on me as it turned out to be. I dragged myself into camp long after everyone else, barely in time to help Brooke finish putting up the tent. The evidence was becoming too plain to ignore. That night, when we were in our sleeping bags, I said, "Listen, there is something I want to talk to you about."

She gave me a curious look. My tone of voice was wrong for 19,000 feet. It was for sea-level subjects, like how were we going to pay for tuition.

"I'm having a tough time," I said.

"Yeah," she said. "So am I. It is a lot harder than I thought it would be."

"You're doing fine," I said. "But I might not make it."

"Sure you will," she insisted.

I shook my head. "Maybe. But it's no sure thing."

She started to say something, but I cut her off.

"Now, listen," I said, going into full father mode, "if I do have to turn around, I want you to keep on going and get to the summit."

"No," she said. "I'm not going if you aren't."

"Yes," I said. "You are. Don't be a kid about this. You've got a shot at it, you've earned it, and you might not ever get it again. You go for it; understand me?"

I spoke to her, not as a grown woman, but the way I had spoken to her when the unstated and unmistakable message was— "And no arguments, young lady." There were 21 years of history in my tone and delivery. It was probably, I thought, the last time I would ever talk to her this way. However this thing turned out, it would be different between us. She wouldn't be my little girl anymore. Not in my mind and certainly not in hers.

She nodded, looking a little hurt.

"Take some pictures and bring me a rock."

She nodded again.

"And don't look so sad. Tomorrow is a rest day; maybe I'll rally."

▲ ▲ ▲

I didn't believe it and neither did she. But we didn't discuss it again. We spent the next day resting, getting our summit packs ready, listening to Jim's briefing on what to expect and acting, in general, as though tomorrow was just another day and that we would both make it to the top, just like we had always imagined it and talked about it. Dads don't get old and little girls don't grow up. Things are just supposed to go on the way they always have—even when they don't.

▲ ▲ ▲

We all went to our tents that night with an edge of nervous anticipation replacing the dull determination that had been the prevailing mood through the last ten days.

The wind blew hard that night and that may have been what kept me awake. But it was probably my gloomy sense that tomorrow, nine people from our group would make it to the summit of Aconcagua while I lay on my back, here in camp. It was a bleak vision made worse by the fact that, of the nine, one would be my daughter. I could barely make myself contemplate the image of her coming back into camp successfully and telling me how it had been.

The wind rose and with it my hope that there would be no summit attempt in the morning. Maybe we'd be trapped in our tents, like the partners of the blonde from Colorado, stuck until our food ran out (we didn't have that much anymore, after all) and we were forced to give it up. If none of us made it, then it would be no special lick on me for giving out at 19,000.

It was an ugly thought and I still had enough shame to feel

guilty for thinking it. Still . . . I lay awake a long time, listening to the wind and wondering if we would even have to get out of our bags in the morning.

▲ ▲ ▲

I hadn't been asleep long when Matt shouted through the tent that it was time to get up. It was 3:30 and the wind was still blowing.

"Get dressed," he said. "We're going for it. If the wind doesn't die down, we'll come back and try again tomorrow."

So we dressed and checked our packs one last time. Ate as much oatmeal as we could choke down, which wasn't more than a spoonful or two in my case, and then started up the mountain, toward the summit, in the dark. The sky was cluttered with stars from horizon to horizon. The wind, I found myself thinking, would fall off at daylight and there wouldn't be any turning around unless you did it on your own.

▲ ▲ ▲

For two hours we trudged along, single file, in the dark, using little battery-powered headlamps for illumination. The wind howled and made the walking that much harder. When I stopped to lean on my ice ax and suck the rarefied air, spectral shapes moved past me in the dark, hoods of parkas pulled over the climbers' heads so they resembled monks in cassocks and the glow off headlamps could have come from candles. Their slow struggle across the loose scree might have been a kind of penance from souls trying to prove themselves worthy of the mountain.

You think strange thoughts in that anemic air.

Two hours after we started, the sun came up. And not long after that, Jim Williams stopped the group until everyone caught up. It was time to put on crampons and make some final, merciless assessments. Some people made their own. Two of the men from our group decided they couldn't make it and turned back for camp. Nobody tried to talk them out of it. They started down the trail we had just come up, looking like they were in a hurry.

Williams spoke to me. "You're not going to make it," he said. It was not a threat or a warning, but a simple statement of fact. At this altitude we were beyond theatrics and pep talks.

Williams had explained the day before that he would give everyone the best possible chance to make the summit. But nobody, he said emphatically, was coming down the mountain in the dark or spending the night in the open. He did not have a turnaround time that was fixed in stone, but he'd know the moment when it came and there would be no arguments. This from a man who had once turned a client around 300 feet from the summit of Everest, giving up his own chance at the summit. In two weeks I had developed total respect for him as a leader.

"Should I go down now?"

"Up to you," he said. "I'm just telling you that the way you're going, you won't make it."

Brooke had joined us and heard that part. "So you're going down?" she said.

"No," I said. "I'll keep going for a while."

"Why," she said, "if you know you're not going to make it?" I could tell she was beginning to worry about the old man. Maybe I would push myself too hard.

"I dunno," I said. "See how far I can get."

I tried to give her the old "what the hell" grin, but I don't think it showed through the balaclava.

With six clients still going for the summit, Williams stayed with the four who were slow and Matt went ahead with two who were stronger. And we continued up the mountain. By mid-morning the wind had died entirely, and the sky was a flawless blue, more vivid than any sky I'd ever seen. Williams had picked a perfect summit day.

A 747 passed overhead, and it seemed close enough that I

could have brought it down with a rock. One of those vagrant, oxygen-starved thoughts. In one Aconcagua account I'd read, the climber had hallucinated up a dialogue with his third-grade teacher. I thought about throwing rocks at jetliners. I also sang the lines from the Monty Python ditty, "I'm a lumberjack," which Brooke had sung on ski lifts when she was younger. And recalled lines from Kipling, a habit I had borrowed from T. S. Eliot.

For it's Tommy this an Tommy that
An Tommy ows your soul
But it's thin red line of heroes
When the drums begin to roll

I walked and rested. Walked and rested.

Brooke moved out ahead of me. Her black and yellow parka reminded me of the yellow jackets that had attacked her when she was a child. I noticed her checking back, now and then, to see if I was still there.

The elastic strap from my goggles seemed exceedingly tight and I had a headache. With no wind, I could have changed to glacier glasses. But that would mean going into my pack and that seemed like such an enormous effort. I stayed with the goggles. And the headache.

Jim and Brooke and the other two in our group stopped ahead of me for lunch. When I caught up with them, I tried to eat and managed to get down half a Power Bar. The banana flavor tasted vile. So I chased it with a cough drop.

Before we started again, Brooke spoke to me. "Jim says you might make it."

I suppose I should have felt a surge of confidence and a new eagerness to get on with it. But I was incapable of that.

I said, "We'll see," and started walking again. I would take a few steps and rest, curled over my ski poles and gasping for air, and when my chest had stopped heaving, I would straighten myself up and do it again. And then, one more time. I moved at the speed of glue.

The afternoon seemed to turn hot. People passed me going up. A Japanese climber. Then a German climber. Then a Polish climber. It was a cosmopolitan day in the slow lane.

Then people began to pass me on their way down. I would say, "Congratulations," panting like an exhausted dog and they would say "Hang in there," and we would keep going in our opposing directions. My head was down most of the time, and at one point I looked up into the face of Matt Goewert, who was coming down with the two clients from our group who had summited.

"Well, well," Matt said, "if it isn't the Eveready Bunny." He had the product wrong, so maybe the altitude was even getting to him.

"You're almost there, just go for it."

"Yeah," I said, gasping, then shook hands with the men who I could only think of as teammates and of whom I felt strangely proud. "Good work, you two."

"Your daughter is just up ahead and looking good," one of them said. "You'll be on the summit in an hour."

"Great," I said. Neither believing nor disbelieving.

"We'll see you in camp."

Someone pounded my shoulder in a gesture of camaraderie that even in my oxygen-starved and fatigued state, I appreciated vastly.

I went on, feeling a little surge.

Oh, I'm a lumberjack
And I'm okay.
I sleep all night.
And I work all day.

I could see the summit and it didn't seem to be getting any closer, though I felt sure I was moving. And I kept moving, though every step seemed to require the kind of effort you would spend walking waist-deep through wet cement. The teeth of one crampon would bite, the sound would serve to reassure me that I had taken another step. Then, with great effort, I'd take another and hear, again, the sound of steel cutting ice. That's how I knew I was moving. But I had no sense of getting any closer. And through the cloud of fatigue and indifference, I began to feel a kind of dread that at any moment Jim Williams would appear before me, the way he had in the storm, and tell me that it was all over. Time to turn around.

And I was so close. It just wasn't fair.

How many times had I heard that from my girls. Brooke or Hadley looking at me with an expression full of little-kid woe and indignation. *No fair, Dad. No fair.*

I was beginning to work up a premature sense of self-pity when I actually heard Williams' voice. Or thought I did. Maybe I was hallucinating. Was this it? Was he turning me around?

"Hey, up here."

I looked up. Williams was leaning over a boulder, maybe 20 feet above me.

"I'm standing on the summit with your daughter," he said. "Why don't you join us."

"Believe I will," I said. "Give me just a minute."

It was more like 10 or 15. Brooke was there with Williams and the two men from our team, and when I made that last step, I gave her a hug.

It had been climbed many times before, and we had taken a route that serious climbers would consider unchallenging, but at that moment Aconcagua was our mountain. We were on the summit. I had followed my daughter to the top, which was not the way I had expected it to be or the way that it had always been. But I surely wouldn't have made it any other way. Or had it any other way, either.

We had done it together. And it felt wonderful.

A Long Descent

We dragged ourselves reluctantly away, taking with us a memory that can never fade and leaving behind "thoughts beyond the reaches of our souls."
—H. W. Tilman, *The Ascent of Nanda Devi*

So in the end, I did not ride out off Aconcagua's slopes on the back of a mule, in disgrace.

Still, it was a long walk down and out. But the company was good and there were moments like the one at our camp at 19,000 feet, an hour or so after I'd gotten down from the summit and was sitting on a rock, stunned and drinking tea. The climber we called the Polish kid made a point of coming by to shake my hand and congratulate me and then shake Brooke's hand and congratulate her. He'd watched us since the second camp on the trek in, and he'd been pulling for us. Probably he thought the odds were long and, with his background, had a weakness for underdogs.

Neither of us suffered any lasting damage, though Brooke's face was so badly sunburned that it had begun weeping at night, and when she woke up, the skin of her cheek would be stuck to the fabric of her sleeping bag. She evidently heard all those lectures about using sunscreen (and drinking plenty of water) but didn't think they applied to fair-skinned blondes. It was, I told her, just like old times, when she was a kid and nobody could tell her anything.

Very funny, she said.

I had sore knees, which was predictable and inevitable and no big deal. Also some minor frostbite in my fingers. Not bad enough to keep me from typing, so also, no big deal.

All the skin on Brooke's face peeled off as soon as she took a hot shower back at the ski lodge. She looked great. My fingers finally stopped tingling about three weeks after we got home, and no one noticed any difference, including me.

Our team had a big dinner celebration along with the group we had shared a bus with on the way out of Santiago three weeks earlier. Two celebrations, in fact. The first was in the dining room of the ski lodge. The second at a Polynesian restaurant in Santiago. There was much wine and some dancing. Matt Goewert danced a hula better than any of the professionals at the night club. I went back to the hotel with one group. Brooke went bar hopping with another. Further evidence, if any was needed, of a changing of the guard.

The next morning, people began drifting out to the airport to make their separate ways home. Brooke and I had a late plane, so we shopped for lapis lazuli jewelry (Santiago is a big source) for Marsha and Hadley and did some sightseeing. We had already called home and Marsha was both relieved and thrilled. Typically, she made more out of the thrilled part, telling us over and over how proud she was of us. Before she gave the phone to Hadley, she made plans for meeting us at the airport and the welcome-home party she would be throwing later in the week.

"You two are so cool," Hadley said, when it was her turn. "Did you bring me a rock?"

Brooke and I told each other—while we were in Santiago, on the plane back, and once we got home—that we had done our big mountain now, that it was finished and behind us. It had been too hard and taken too long for us even to think about doing it again. We sorted through the duffels—which had a peculiar, indelible scent—and then put them away, deep in an upstairs crawl space. Brooke went back to school and I went back to work, and we went back to communicating by phone and e-mail instead of talking every day, sometimes all day, and over the sound of a hard wind pounding the sides of a nylon tent.

We recalled some of our moments together on Aconcagua in these conversations and talked about climbing in general. One day I had to call her and tell her about the news I had heard from a shocked friend: Alex Lowe had been killed in a freak avalanche in the Himalayas.

Brooke was stunned, as I had been. You know, even if you are just a novice, that climbers die. But not that climber. Not Alex Lowe.

"His poor kids," Brooke said.

▲ ▲ ▲

As it always does, however, the death of a climber becomes something that you accept and assign utterly to the past. If climbing accidents were enough to persuade climbers to quit, then the mountains would never be crowded. A couple of months after the news about Lowe, I said something in one of our phone conversations about maybe looking for another mountain to climb.

Brooke told me to take a walk back in my mind and remember how it had been at 19,000 feet, when we were putting up our tent in that storm.

I see what you're driving at, I said.

Then, a couple of months after that, we were talking again and she brought up the subject.

"You know," she said, "I kind of miss it."

"Me, too," I said.

"Maybe," she said, "we could do another big one together sometime."

"I don't see why not," I said. "Just one. But soon. Before you get too busy and I get too old."